VIVIAN ROBINSON Q
TRUMAN K. BUTLER
AUTHORS

THE FCPA AND U.K. BRIBERY ACT

A READY REFERENCE FOR BUSINESS AND LAWYERS

REVISED AND UPDATED

Printed in the United States of America.

23 22 21 20 19   5 4 3 2 1

ISBN: 978-1-64105-546-8

Discounts are available for books ordered in bulk. Special consideration is given to state bars, CLE programs, and other bar-related organizations. Inquire at Book Publishing, ABA Publishing, American Bar Association, 321 N. Clark Street, Chicago, Illinois 60654-7598.

www.ShopABA.org

Contents

APPENDIX A

Excerpt - A Resource Guide To The U.S. Foreign Corrupt Practices Act ('FCPA Resource Guide') 83

APPENDIX B

Excerpt - The Bribery Act 2010: Guidance about procedures which relevant commercial organisations can put into place to prevent persons associated with them from bribing (section 9 of the Bribery Act 2010) ('Government Guidance')

About the Authors

Vivian Robinson QC

Vivian Robinson QC advises clients on the UK Bribery Act, as well as compliance on white-collar crime matters involving global fraud or corruption, including the Foreign Corrupt Practices Act ('FCPA'). As former first General Counsel to the UK's Serious Fraud Office ('SFO'), he led the development of the SFO's enforcement policy under the UK Bribery Act. He also served as the SFO's primary liaison with the business community to the UK Bribery Act's requirements at conferences in London, New York and other parts of the world.

Mr. Robinson became a barrister in 1967 and practised at the English criminal bar for over forty years, acting for both prosecution and defence. He was appointed Queen's Counsel in 1986, was elected Head of QEB Hollis Whiteman Chambers in 2006 and served as the Treasurer of the Inner Temple in 2009. He first sat as a part-time judge over thirty years ago and continues to do so. In 2009 he left the practising bar to take an appointment as first General Counsel at the SFO.

In 2011 he was invited to join the US law firm McGuireWoods, where he practices in London as a member of the firm's Government, Regulatory and Criminal Investigation team. Since joining the firm, he has travelled extensively speaking on the UK Bribery Act and related issues. He is a graduate of Sidney Sussex College, Cambridge University, BA (Cantab.)

Stuart H. Deming

Stuart H. Deming represents and advises clients on the FCPA, the UK Bribery Act, Canada's Corruption of Foreign Public Officials Act and other compliance issues associated with the conduct of international business. As a former federal prosecutor with the U.S. Securities and Exchange Commission and in various capacities with the U.S. Department of Justice, including as a special prosecutor, he led investigations of major companies, business executives and public officials.

With over thirty years of experience in both the public and private sector, Mr. Deming has written extensively and spoken often in the US and abroad on the FCPA and related issues. He is the author of Oxford University Press' ANTI-BRIBERY LAWS IN COMMON LAW JURISDICTIONS; the ABA's DESIGNING AN EFFECTIVE ANTI-BRIBERY COMPLIANCE PROGRAM: A PRACTICAL GUIDE FOR BUSINESS; and the ABA's THE FOREIGN CORRUPT PRACTICES ACT AND THE NEW INTERNATIONAL NORMS.

For many years Mr. Deming co-chaired the ABA's National Institutes on the FCPA; he founded and co-chaired what is now the ABA's Anti-Corruption Committee; and he served on the Board of Editorial Advisors to the FOREIGN CORRUPT PRACTICES ACT REPORTER. Mr. Deming received his BA, MBA, and JD from the University of Michigan. He is also licensed as a Certified Public Accountant.

Truman K. Butler

Truman K. Butler is an international transactions attorney who has been actively involved with a range of compliance issues for major financial services firms. His practice includes providing advice on international compliance matters including the FCPA, UK Bribery Act, anti-money laundering laws and global sanctions. He most recently served as the Head of Global Risk & Compliance Assurance at a major biopharmaceutical corporation.

Mr. Butler's professional experience spans private practice, financial services firms and life sciences. He has served as Senior Counsel with the Anti-Laundering, Global Sanctions and Anti-Corruption team of a global financial services firm, including as Assistant General Counsel responsible for international commercial transactions of a predecessor financial services firm. He previously served as corporate counsel at Lloyds TSB Bank International with responsibility for commercial transactions and corporate compliance in Latin America and the Caribbean.

Licensed in England and Wales as a Barrister at Law of the Middle Temple, Mr. Butler is also licenced in the US in North Carolina and the

Commonwealth of The Bahamas. An active member of the ABA's Section of International Law, he is a former Co-Chair of the International Anti-Money Laundering Committee and a former Steering Group Member of the International Anti-Corruption Committee. He received his LLB from the University of Wolverhampton, England and his LLM from the University of Georgia.

Preface

This booklet has been specifically written for laypersons and, in particular, for business people as well as lawyers with limited experience. Our objective was to provide a concise and useful explanation of the US Foreign Corrupt Practices Act ('FCPA') and the UK Bribery Act along with helpful guidance as to what entities should be doing to minimize their risk of legal liability.

We believe this booklet will be useful to any entity. This includes the traditional for-profit entities like companies and partnerships as well as non-profit entities such as non-governmental organisations. Given the broad reach of the FCPA and the UK Bribery Act, and the implications of a host of other legal regimes, this booklet is also highly relevant to foreign entities not generally perceived as being subject to either statute.

The phrase, often attributed to George Bernard Shaw, that the US and UK are 'two nations divided by a common language' has often come to mind in the course of our efforts. For consistency, English spelling and punctuation has therefore been used. Yet in terms of substance, both a US and UK perspective has been carefully maintained throughout our joint efforts.

Chapter 1
Introduction

By its enactment of the Foreign Corrupt Practices Act ('FCPA') in 1977, the United States ('US') became the first country to prohibit the bribery of foreign public officials ('FPO'). Prior to that time, no country prohibited the bribery of FPOs. Indeed, the bribery of FPOs was so much an accepted practice that it was recognized by taxing authorities in most of the world as a legitimate business expense. Through a series of rather dramatic international developments beginning in the 1990s, that has all changed.

Today most developed countries have implemented and increasingly enforce their domestic legislation prohibiting the bribery of FPOs. Virtually all other countries are parties to international conventions prohibiting the bribery of FPOs. It is only a matter of time before most of the world will have adopted domestic legislation prohibiting the bribery of FPOs.

With the aggressive enforcement by the US, and by reason of its very terms, the global reach of the FCPA has been far greater than any other anti-bribery statute. Compliance with the FCPA must be a focus for entities engaged in international business. But, in addition, the breadth and global reach of the UK's Bribery Act 2010 ('UK Bribery Act') now effectively requires entities engaged in international business to also comply with its terms.

As a practical matter, the FCPA and the UK Bribery Act can apply to almost anyone engaged in international business. Often in unexpected ways, entities, or anyone acting on their behalf, can become subject to prosecution for violating either law. The possibilities are virtually endless. As opposed to determining when either law may apply, an entity's efforts are better directed towards understanding each law and how best to avoid a violation.

This booklet seeks to provide management and key personnel with a clear and concise explanation of the FCPA and the UK Bribery Act. In addition, since the US and the UK have increasingly employed a number of ancillary laws to address the bribery of FPOs, attention will be given to these other laws and how they may relate to conduct involving the payment of bribes in foreign settings.

Given the scope of these prohibitions, by complying with the FCPA and the UK Bribery Act, an entity will be more assured of complying with the array of anti-bribery laws increasingly being enforced in much of the world. Having a sense of these corresponding provisions will also provide further insight as to the steps that entities need to take to ensure compliance.

Chapter 2
Foreign Corrupt Practices Act

Through the FCPA, the US Congress sought to deter foreign corrupt practices—specifically the offer or payment of anything of value to FPOs in connection with business activities—through two principal mechanisms: the anti-bribery provisions and the accounting and record-keeping provisions. The two sets of provisions are conceptually different from each other. The former is proscriptive in orientation, and the latter is prescriptive. Their scope and application are also different.

Essential to any analysis of a situation that may involve an FCPA violation is the consideration of whether the anti-bribery provisions or the accounting and record-keeping provisions, or both, may be involved. A certain set of facts may suggest a violation of the anti-bribery provisions yet may not suggest a violation of the accounting and record-keeping provisions. Each set of provisions must be considered separately. At the same time, neither provision should be considered alone. They were intended to work in tandem and thereby complement one another.

A. The Anti-Bribery Provisions

The anti-bribery provisions prohibit improper inducements to FPOs. An improper inducement is any promise, offer or payment of anything of value if the person making the promise, offer or payment knows that a portion will be used for the purpose of influencing the conduct of an FPO.

1. Scope and Application

While the FCPA applies directly to certain categories of individuals and entities, the ways in which an individual or entity can be indirectly subject to liability under the FCPA are almost endless. For this reason, regardless of whether an individual or entity is directly subject to the anti-bribery provisions of the FCPA, any individual or entity engaged in international business must assume that he or she, or it, may be subject to the anti-bribery provisions of the FCPA.

a. Any Person

The anti-bribery provisions apply to both individuals and entities as long as they are issuers, domestic concerns or they cause an act in furtherance of an improper inducement to take place within the territory of the US. The only other consideration is whether an individual or entity is a *US person*.

(1) US Person

To be a 'US person', an individual must be a US citizen or national. For an entity, a US person is an entity organised under the laws of the US, which includes the laws of any state, territory, possession, commonwealth or any subdivision of each. Based solely on an individual's or entity's status as a US person, it makes no difference whether his, her or its involvement has absolutely no connection to the US. The anti-bribery provisions apply to that individual or entity regardless of geographic location or relationship to the US.

(2) All Other Individuals or Entities

For any individual or entity that is not a US person, in order for the anti-bribery provisions to apply, the individual or entity must use the mails or means or instrumentality of interstate or foreign commerce of the US in furtherance of an improper inducement. Given widespread use of telecommunications, the internet, air travel, and other forms of communication as well as modes of making payments, it will be a relatively rare situation where some form of means or instrumentality of interstate or foreign commerce of the US is not used in furtherance of an improper inducement.

b. Accomplices

Regardless of whether an individual or entity is subject to the anti-bribery provisions, an individual or entity can become liable as an accomplice to a violation of the anti-bribery provisions. This can occur when an entity or individual acts as an aider or abettor or as a conspirator to a violation.

(1) Aiders and Abettors

An aider and abettor can be subject to a statutory violation even if that individual or entity cannot be charged directly with violating the statute. Nor is the prosecution of an aider and abettor barred when the principal has been acquitted. To be liable as an aider and abettor, an individual or entity must act with *intent that the offence be committed.*

An individual or entity need not actually violate the anti-bribery provisions. It is the conduct on the part of an individual or entity to assist another party's violation that may serve as the basis for liability as an accomplice. Moreover, an individual or entity not directly subject to the anti-bribery provisions may be exposed to liability as an aider and abettor of an individual or entity subject to the anti-bribery provisions.

(2) Conspirators

Except generally for FPOs, persons not otherwise liable under the anti-bribery provisions may, depending upon the circumstances, be prosecuted for conspiring to violate their provisions. A conspiracy is established when two or more persons combine or agree to violate a federal statute. If one member acts in furtherance of the conspiracy before the other indicates withdrawal from the conspiracy, both can be held criminally liable for having entered into the conspiracy.

When a conspiracy to violate the anti-bribery provisions is involved, no improper inducement needs to be offered or made. It is the **agreement** to violate the anti-bribery provisions that serves as the basis for the criminal charge. The only additional requirement is that there be an overt act by one of the co-conspirators in furtherance of the conspiracy to violate the anti-bribery provisions. Rather insignificant activity can meet this additional requirement.

2. Essential Elements

The anti-bribery provisions are expansive and designed to preclude any means of circumventing their terms. Except for a few narrow exceptions, the anti-bribery provisions of the FCPA have been consistently applied in an expansive manner by the U.S. Department of Justice ('Justice Department') and U.S. Securities and Exchange Commission ('SEC') to preclude any means of avoiding their terms.

a. Payment, Offer or Promise

It makes no difference if a payment is actually made. Nor does it matter whether an offer or promise is ever fulfilled. Any offer or promise that could reasonably be believed to be an improper inducement is prohibited. Nor is there a requirement that the FPO accept the bribe. Similarly, there is no requirement that anyone actually receive the bribe or that the object of the bribe actually be attainable. All that is required is that what is paid, offered or promised be sufficient to form the basis for an improper inducement.

It also makes no difference how an improper payment, offer or promise is made. Any improper inducement made indirectly or through intermediaries is prohibited. No matter how attenuated a payment, offer or promise may be made or communicated to its intended recipient, any indirect means of making or communicating a prohibited inducement may be the basis for a violation of the anti-bribery provisions. The manner or means by which a payment, promise or offer is made cannot provide a safe harbour or the basis of a defence.

(1) Authorisation

The anti-bribery provisions also prohibit the 'authorisation' of an improper inducement to be made by another. To authorise means to give approval or direction to carry out conduct. Authorisation in the form of acquiescence or direction can be implicit and can be derived from a course of conduct that conveys an intent that an improper inducement be made.

Depending upon the nature of the relationship between the individual or entity and the third party, and the surrounding circumstances, acquiescence may constitute authorisation. Authorisation may also entail knowing acquiescence or tacit approval by individuals or entities that might have prevented the conduct that led to the making of an improper inducement. For example, conscious acquiescence to a series of unauthorised acts could be found to constitute authorisation to engage in similar acts in the future.

Ratification of conduct that leads to the making of improper inducements may also serve as a basis for liability. If a foreign partner has already made improper payments to FPOs, capital contributions by a domestic concern or issuer could be regarded as a reimbursement of the improper payments. Distributions by a joint venture could also have the same effect. In both instances, the domestic concern or issuer would have had to know of the previous improper payments made by the foreign partner.

An issuer or a domestic concern can be liable for the conduct of its foreign subsidiary if it in some way directs, authorises or knowingly acquiesces to prohibited conduct on the part of the foreign subsidiary. In such circumstances, the failure to address the prohibited conduct may be construed as an implicit authorisation of the prohibited conduct.

Whether an entity owns less than a controlling interest in a foreign affiliate is not determinative for establishing liability for the actions taken on the part of the foreign affiliate. Practical or effective control can still be exercised even with an interest less than 50 percent. When an individual or entity has a controlling interest or effective control, it is more likely to become aware of the prohibited conduct.

(2) Requisite Knowledge

An individual or entity is responsible for the conduct of a third party when an individual or entity 'knew' that the money or thing of value given to the third party would be used, directly or indirectly, to make an improper payment. *Actual knowledge is not required.* An individual or entity is deemed to have the requisite knowledge of an activity by a third party if the individual or entity:

- is aware that such person is engaging in such conduct, that such circumstance exists, or that *such result is substantially certain to occur*; or

- has a *firm belief* that such circumstance exists or that *such result is substantially certain to occur.*

The knowledge standard applies to situations where there is a conscious disregard, wilful blindness or deliberate ignorance of circumstances that should alert one to the likelihood of a violation of the anti-bribery provisions. When confronted with circumstances that should normally raise suspicions in a particular context, or what are often referred to as 'red flags', knowledge on the part of an individual or entity is more likely to be inferred.

When an individual or entity becomes aware of questionable circumstances regarding the activities of a third party, steps should be taken to address the questionable circumstances. Otherwise, an individual or entity could be found to have consciously disregarded information that served as notice of the likelihood of a violation. Failure to inquire could result in the imputation to an individual or entity of knowledge regarding the prohibited conduct.

b. Anything of Value

As the phrase 'anything of value' suggests, what is given or offered can be as broad and as esoteric as can be reasonably conceived. In addition to cash or some form of monetary instrument, *almost any form of direct or indirect benefit could constitute something of value.* This might include a benefit to a family member or a right or ability to designate to whom a benefit is directed.

No limitations exist on what can be construed as 'anything of value'. Among the benefits that have typically been viewed as falling within the prohibitions of the anti-bribery provisions are scholarships and internships for family members, upgrades to first-class airfare, side trips to resorts and permitting an official to designate to whom charitable contributions are directed.

What may be of value may depend upon the circumstances. How a potential benefit is apt to be perceived by the intended recipient is critical. In this regard, what may be perceived as inconsequential in one setting may be perceived as significant in other settings. For someone of limited means, what may comprise value could be perceived quite differently for someone of substantial means.

Because *the anti-bribery provisions have no de minimis exception*, the context in which the inducement is made may be determinative of what constitutes 'anything of value'. For example, where certain natural resources are limited, like access to water in an arid region, providing access to such limited resources could be of significant value. In other contexts, such as in a region with an abundance of water, providing access to water may not be of much significance.

c. Foreign Public Official ('FPO')

Who is considered an FPO under the anti-bribery provisions should be presumed to have as broad an application as possible. Who is an FPO is not dependent on whether the individual is classified as an FPO under foreign law. A critical factor in determining whether someone is an FPO is whether the individual occupies a position of public trust with official responsibilities.

Regardless of country, the prohibitions apply to officials of all branches of government as well as to all units of government. This includes civil service and political functions in countries where those functions are not unified. It does not matter whether the FPO is a paid or an unpaid official.

(1) Political Parties, Party Officials or Candidates for Public Office

Political parties, party officials or any candidate for public office are specifically included within the prohibitions of the anti-bribery provisions. A precise definition is not provided as to what constitutes a candidate for public office. Given the expansive manner in which the anti-bribery provisions have been applied, formalisms such as an announced candidacy should not be assumed to be determinative.

Whether an individual actually holds a position as a party official also may not be determinative. The practical realities of the particular individual's status within a political party may ultimately be more determinative. Perceptions of an individual's influence will be critical to any assessment. For example, a payment to a retired senior party leader may be equivalent to a payment to a party official because of his or her role behind the scenes.

(2) De Facto *Members of Government*

The line between what does and does not constitute an FPO can become especially blurred when members of royal families may be involved. One classic situation may be in the Middle East where, in some countries, the royal families are large and their unofficial roles in affairs of state can be significant. On the other extreme, in many European countries members of royal families play no meaningful role in governing.

Mere status as a member of a royal family does not make an individual an FPO. Depending upon the facts, members of a royal family may be considered an FPO within the meaning of the anti-bribery provisions, regardless of whether the family members have official titles or positions. Of particular importance is the ability that a member of a royal family may have to affect, even in an indirect manner, a decision by a member or unit of government.

Among the many other factors to consider include:

- The manner in which power is exercised and distributed within a country;
- The current and historical legal status and powers of a royal family;
- The individual's position within the royal family as well as past and present governmental positions; and
- The manner, and likelihood, by which an individual can hold or succeed to a position with governmental authority or responsibilities.

(3) State-Owned or State-Controlled Entities

The anti-bribery provisions apply to 'instrumentalities' of foreign governments, often referred to as 'parastatals' or state-owned or state-controlled entities or enterprises. The result is that an FPO under the anti-bribery provisions may include someone who is employed by a commercial enterprise owned or operated by a unit of government or carrying out a public function.

Depending upon the country, or even certain parts of a country, whether the services are provided by government can vary. Traditionally, what are often viewed as commercial enterprises can also be state-owned or state-controlled in some settings. State-owned or state-controlled enterprises are generally more apt to be present in business sectors that involve aerospace and defence manufacturing, banking and finance, telecommunications, transportation, energy and extractive industries, health care and life sciences, and sanitation services. But the range of activities in which a state-owned or state-controlled entity may be engaged are virtually unlimited.

The likelihood that an entity will be considered state-owned or state-controlled is increased with the degree to which a country is or has been socialised. As privatisation takes place in various parts of the world, the likelihood that entities will be considered state-owned or state-controlled will diminish. Similarly, the greater the degree to which nationalisation takes place, the likelihood that an entity may be considered state-owned or state-controlled entities will increase. The incidence of state-owned or state-controlled will vary over time with the political dynamics of a country. Yet nothing should be assumed. What may appear to be a traditional commercial enterprise may, in reality, be state-owned or state-controlled.

As suggested by the Justice Department and SEC's FCPA Resource Guide, no definitive test exists for determining what constitutes a state-owned or state-controlled entity under the anti-bribery provisions. A critical factor will be the degree to which a government or governments may, directly or indirectly, exercise a dominant influence. Dominant influence may be demonstrated in a number of ways such as:

- When the foreign government holds a majority of an entity's subscribed capital;
- When the foreign government controls the majority of the votes of shares issued by the entity; or
- When the foreign government or an FPO can appoint a majority of the enterprise's administrative or managerial body or supervisory board.

A related consideration is whether exclusive or controlling power is vested in the entity to administer its designated functions.

Another critical factor is what the purpose of an entity's activities may be. Along these lines, other factors that may bear upon whether an entity is state-owned or state-controlled include:

- Whether and the degree to which an entity carries out a public function;

- Whether and the degree to which an entity may have 'obligations and privileges under the foreign state's law';
- Whether and, if so, how an entity is characterized by its government;
- Whether the foreign government prohibits and prosecutes bribery of the employees of state-owned or state-controlled entities;
- Whether, and to what degree, the foreign unit of government provides financial support, 'including subsidies, special tax treatments, government-mandated fees, and loans';
- Whether the circumstances surrounding the establishment of an entity may be suggestive as to its status;
- Whether the entity provides services to residents within its jurisdiction;
- Whether the governmental end or purpose sought to be achieved is expressed in the policies of the foreign government; or
- Whether there is a general perception that the entity is performing official or governmental functions.

(4) International Organisations

An FPO includes any official or employee of a public international organisation or any individual or entity acting on behalf of a public international organisation. The public international organisations covered by the anti-bribery provisions are those organisations whose officials are accorded diplomatic immunity under US law or that have been designated by the President of the US as an international organisation for purposes of the anti-bribery provisions.

The mechanism by which organisations are accorded diplomatic immunity is by executive order pursuant to the International Organizations Immunities Act. Organisations as diverse as the Organization of American States, the European Space Agency and the Hong Kong Economic and Trade Offices are currently listed. Over time, this list can be expected to grow. Unless a definitive determination is made, prudence suggests that inducements to or for the benefit of any official or employee of any international organisation, or any individual or entity acting on behalf of an international organisation, should be presumed to be prohibited.

d. Corrupt Intent

An improper inducement occurs only when an payment or offer of payment is made to induce the intended beneficiary to in some way misuse his or her official position. The individual or entity must have a bad or wrongful purpose and an intent to influence an FPO to misuse his or her official position. The thing of value must be given or offered with the *intent to influence* as opposed to be simply given whether or not the FPO carries out his or her official duties. The improper inducement must be the prime mover or producer of the official act.

(1) Knowledge and Intent of Inducer is the Sole Consideration

Culpability is determined by the *intent of the person making the inducement* as opposed to the FPO's action, inaction or capacity. It is not relevant whether the FPO has the capacity to influence an official decision. Even if a payment or offer is 'intended to influence an official act that was lawful', there would still be a violation.

The payment or offer need not be accepted in order for there to be a violation. Nor does the intended beneficiary need to have the actual authority to make or influence the official decision. It is also not relevant whether an inducement is made directly or indirectly to an FPO.

(2) Knowledge and Intent of an Entity

The knowledge requirement under US law for an entity is distinctly different from that of an individual. It is far different than most countries. Indeed, the threshold for establishing knowledge on the part of an entity is much easier to prove than virtually any other country in the world.

Under US law, no one person within an entity must have the requisite knowledge. Nor is there a requirement that there be knowledge on the part of senior members of management. Regardless of how disparate the knowledge may be within an entity, the collective knowledge of employees and agents acting within the scope of their duties can serve as the basis for establishing knowledge under US law. In short, it is the sum of the knowledge of an entity's officers, directors, employees and agents, when acting within the scope of their employment or responsibilities, that establishes knowledge on the part of an entity.

As a result, actions on the part of isolated members of management or on the part of low-level employees can expose an entity to liability. Even more likely is the prospect of lower-level employees or isolated members of management having knowledge of prohibited conduct being undertaken by third parties on behalf of an entity. In such circumstances, the failure of an entity to address the prohibited conduct has the prospect of being interpreted as an authorisation or acquiescence on the part of the entity.

e. Influencing an Official Act

Official action or inaction that is sought to be induced to assist in obtaining or retaining business is known as the *quid pro quo* element of the anti-bribery provisions. The types of inducements that are sought to be prohibited fall into four categories:

1. Influencing the FPO's action in the context of the individual's official capacity;
2. Inducing the FPO to do or not to do an act in violation of the individual's lawful duty;
3. Inducing the FPO to influence or affect an act or decision of his or her government; or
4. Securing any improper advantage.

It is not necessary that the action being induced relates to the FPO's government. As long as the action being influenced relates to the official capacity of the individual being induced, the ultimate purpose need not relate to the FPO's government or to any government. For example, inducing an FPO to put in a 'good word' with the US Government relative to a procurement opportunity by a US firm has served as a basis for enforcement action.

f. To Obtain or Retain Business

The anti-bribery provisions prohibit inducements to an FPO in order to assist the individual or entity in obtaining or retaining business for or with, or directing business to, any individual or entity. The inducement must be intended to induce the FPO to act on the inducer's behalf to assist the individual or entity making the inducement in obtaining or retaining business.

The anti-bribery provisions extend to official acts or inaction that indirectly assist the individual or entity making the inducement. Inducements seeking official action favourable to carrying on a business enterprise satisfy the business purpose element of the anti-bribery provisions. This includes making it easier to do more business.

The term 'assist' in the anti-bribery provisions has been given a broad interpretation. Various actions can assist a particular goal simply by making the eventual realization of that goal more likely. This might include payments to circumvent quotas, bypass licensing requirements, obtain concessions or reduce taxes. In so doing, an improper inducement assists in obtaining or retaining business by increasing the amount of product available for sale or reducing an inducer's expenses of sale. This could extend, for example, to increasing or maintaining the quantity of its sales or other economic dealings.

No requirement exists for the FPO to be directly involved in awarding or directing the business. Retaining business is not limited to the renewal of contracts or other business. The prohibition extends to more than the renewal or award of a contract. It extends to corrupt payments related to the execution or performance of a contract or the carrying out of existing business. It also extends to payments to an FPO for the purpose of obtaining more favourable treatment.

Activities of a non-profit or charitable organisation are equally subject to the terms of the anti-bribery provisions. If established under US law or if its principal place of business is in the US, a non-profit or charitable organisation is a domestic concern for purposes of the anti-bribery provisions. For example, regardless of what the laudable purpose of a non-profit or charitable organisation may be, an improper inducement that would permit such an organisation to become established in a country should be presumed to be subject to the terms of the anti-bribery provisions.

3. Exceptions, Affirmative Defences and Related Considerations

Relief from application of the anti-bribery provisions is limited. Yet there are a few categories of circumstances where inducements may be permitted. The practical effect is to provide a form of safe harbour for limited categories of inducements that would otherwise be prohibited by the anti-bribery provisions.

a. Statute of Limitations

The statute of limitations associated with the enforcement of the anti-bribery provisions is five years. This applies in both a criminal and a civil enforcement context.

Reliance solely upon a five-year statute of limitations as a basis for determining whether action will be taken can be misplaced. Capable enforcement officials can come up with legitimate ways of extending the five-year limitation period. The statute of limitations may have in some way been tolled or suspended; evidence may be discovered suggesting a continuing offence; or alternative legal theories may be employed.

In a civil context, for individuals not resident in the US, the statute of limitations period is also deemed to be tolled or suspended for any period the individual is not 'found' within the US where proper service may be made.

b. Facilitating Payments

Through an exception, the anti-bribery provisions permit what are commonly referred to as facilitating payments. These payments are made to *expedite* or to secure the performance of a *routine* governmental action by an FPO. Expediting payments are given to secure or accelerate performance of a nondiscretionary act that an FPO is already obligated to perform.

(1) Nondiscretionary Act

A facilitating payment relates to actions on the part of FPOs that are not discretionary in nature. For example, if the issuance of a permit is deemed to be automatic or only a matter of time, it is not subject to discretion. A payment made to expedite the process or move the issuance of a permit up in line is likely to be considered a facilitating payment. A payment to a government-run telephone company to expedite installation of service is also apt to be considered a facilitating payment. No question exists as to whether one can get the telephone service; the payment is intended only to influence the timing.

Routine governmental action includes only action that is *ordinarily and commonly* performed by an FPO. It does not include any decision by an FPO to award new business or to continue business. Facilitating payments can include payments made to obtain permits, licences, or other official documents and to receive services such as police protection, mail, telephone, utilities, cargo handling and the protection of perishable products. They also include payments made in exchange for the processing of governmental papers, including visas and work orders; scheduling of inspections associated with contract performance or the transit of goods across a country; and expediting shipments through customs.

(2) Need for Caution

Determining what constitutes a facilitation payment can be extremely difficult. It is highly dependent upon the circumstances. What may be perceived as a facilitating payment under one set of circumstances may not be similarly perceived under another set of circumstances.

The value of what is offered or paid is not necessarily determinative. Typically, facilitating payments are *de minimis* in terms of value. In theory, a large amount of money could still be determined to be a facilitating payment. However, the greater the value of a facilitating payment, the less likely will the payment be perceived as being a facilitating payment.

Particular caution needs to be exercised with respect to the use of facilitating payments. Facilitating payments are seldom, if ever, permitted by the written law of a host country. The individual who makes the payment, as well as those who authorised it, may be subject to criminal liability in the host country. In addition, the implications associated with starting down a 'slippery slope' justifying suspect payments must always be kept carefully in mind when facilitating payments are made.

c. Bona Fide *Business Expenditures*

Reasonable and *bona fide* expenditures are permitted. To be permitted, the expenditures must directly relate to the promotion, demonstration or explanation of products or services or to the execution or performance of a contract with a foreign government or agency. When the very essence of these expenditures represents a form of sales promotion, the line can become blurred as to what constitutes a *bona fide* expenditure and what may be perceived as an improper inducement.

(1) Whether Permitted by the FPO's Government

At the outset of any determination of what constitutes a *bona fide* business expenditure, a threshold determination needs to be made concerning whether an FPO or unit of government can be paid or reimbursed for expenses that may be incurred. In many countries, there are limitations on what can be paid and, if so, how such payments are made. Similarly, there may be a need for prior approvals by an FPO's government.

(2) Reasonable Business Expenses

Care must be exercised in determining whether an expenditure is legitimate. Diversions to resorts and travel upgrades to first class can be a cause for concern. It has not been considered a defence that all prospective customers, whether from the private or public sector, are treated the same way. The question is whether the expenditures in each situation are necessary business expenditures and, if so, whether what is paid is reasonable under the circumstances. An expenditure that is out of proportion or unrelated to a legitimate business purpose may serve as a basis for concern.

With the differences in living standards in various parts of the world, situations may arise where relatively modest expenditures can be viewed as improper inducements. In those circumstances, there is a heightened need to be able to justify the legitimate basis for the expenditures that are made. Customary practices in certain parts of the world may be viewed as once-in-a-lifetime opportunities in other parts of the world. A variety of perspectives must be kept in mind when determining whether a *bona fide* expenditure is proper.

d. Local Law

An affirmative defence exists, under the anti-bribery provisions, for payments or offers that are lawful under the written laws and regulations of the country of the FPO. It is a rare situation where a government, as an official matter, permits payments or offers of payments to violate a lawful duty. Recognised customs or practices within a particular country cannot form the basis of an affirmative defence. Nor is it a defence if it is a local practice or 'everyone does it'.

The critical factor is whether the practice of making payments to the officials of a country is *permitted* under the *written* laws of the country where the payment is made. Written judicial decisions forming the basis of law in common law jurisdictions would also constitute written law. In most situations, this affirmative defence has little practical relevance. It is most likely to be relevant in situations where contributions to political parties or candidates for public office are involved.

e. Opinion Procedure

There is a procedure, known as the Foreign Corrupt Practices Act Opinion Procedure, by which an issuer or a domestic concern can request an opinion of the Justice Department's enforcement intentions regarding proposed business conduct. The opinion procedure provides a rebuttable presumption that the conduct that is the subject of the opinion does not violate the anti-bribery provisions. An opinion binds only the Justice Department and the parties to a request. *It does not protect anyone else.*

The opinion request should focus only on well-defined issues involving prospective conduct. The Justice Department's opinion will only apply to those portions of the transaction or activity in question that remain prospective. A request must 'be specific and must be accompanied by all relevant and material information bearing on the conduct' for which the opinion is requested. The identities of the parties as well as the particulars of a proposed transaction must be disclosed.

Disclosure must be full and entirely forthcoming. Providing incomplete or inaccurate information can serve as an independent basis for prosecution. The Justice Department may request supplemental information. The Justice Department also has the power to conduct 'whatever independent investigation it believes appropriate' in connection with the request. An opinion will be issued in the 30 days from when the Justice Department receives all the information it requires.

f. Duress

Generally, an individual or entity forced to make an improper inducement under coercion or duress may be able to assert a defence based on coercion or duress. Coercion or duress is established by proving three discrete elements:

1. a threat of force directed *at the time* of the defendant's conduct;
2. a threat sufficient to induce a *well-founded* fear of impending death or serious bodily injury; and
3. a *lack of a reasonable opportunity to escape* harm other than by engaging in the illegal activity.

Limited authority also exists for the proposition that a defence may exist where an individual or entity responds to a situation involving 'true extortion'. This would not extend to situations where an improper inducement is demanded to obtain or retain business. But it may apply in rare situations where a payment is made to avoid a situation like the imminent destruction of valuable property.

4. Sanctions

An individual or entity can be subject to both criminal and civil liability under the anti-bribery provisions. The quantum of proof required is the basis for the difference. For a criminal conviction, proof must be established beyond a reasonable doubt. To establish a civil violation, the standard of proof is only a preponderance of the evidence.

a. Criminal Sanctions

A criminal violation may result in a fine of $2 million per violation for an entity. An individual may face up to five years in prison or a fine of $100,000, or both, for each violation. Fines can be far greater under the alternative sentencing provisions. If there is a pecuniary loss to an individual or entity other than the defendant, the fine can be the greater of twice the gross gain or twice the gross loss.

Fines imposed cannot be paid by an employer or principal. Nor can fines imposed on an entity that serves as an agent or stockholder of an individual or entity subject to the FCPA be paid or reimbursed by its principal.

(1) US Sentencing Guidelines

Regardless of the statutory provisions, an important consideration in terms of a likely criminal penalty are the US Federal Sentencing Guidelines. A complex matrix is provided by the US Federal Sentencing Guidelines for determining fines based upon the culpability of the offender. The relevant factors in assessing culpability include the history of prior violations, the pecuniary gain obtained and the steps taken by the offender to prevent violations such as implementing and enforcing an effective compliance programme.

(2) Critical Components of Effective Compliance Programmes

A compliance programme must be tailored to address the particular risks that are unique to each entity and the nature of an entity's operations. To be effective, they must constantly evolve and adjust as an entity changes as well as the risks that it may encounter. 'A well-constructed, thoughtfully implemented, and consistently enforced compliance and ethics program helps prevent, detect, remediate, and report misconduct, including FCPA violations'.

Compliance programmes can vary depending upon factors unique to each entity and the nature of its business. Risks should be assessed and addressed in a good faith manner. Mechanisms that represent not much more than a 'check-the-box' approach should be avoided. In the FCPA Resource Guide issued by the Justice Department and SEC, a number of 'hallmarks' of an effective compliance programme are identified:

(a) Commitment from Senior Management and a Clearly-Articulated Policy against Corruption

An effective compliance programme requires senior management to have 'clearly articulated company standards, communicated them in unambiguous terms, adhered to them scrupulously, and disseminated them throughout the organization'.

(b) Code of Conduct and Compliance Policies and Procedures

Effective codes of conduct 'are clear, concise, and accessible to all employees and to those conducting business on the company's behalf.' It must be conveyed in the local language. In tailoring policies and procedures to circumstances associated with an entity and the business it conducts, a compliance programme should 'outline responsibilities for compliance within the company, detail proper internal controls, auditing practices, and documentation policies, and set forth disciplinary procedures'.

(c) Oversight, Autonomy, and Resources

In addition to ensuring that there is 'adequate staffing and resources', one or more specific senior members of management should be designated and assigned responsibility of overseeing and implementing a compliance programme. The senior executive should have 'adequate autonomy from management, and sufficient resources to ensure that the company's compliance programme is implemented effectively'. 'Adequate autonomy generally includes direct access to an organization's governing authority, such as the board of directors and committees of the board of directors'.

(d) Risk Assessment

Depending upon the degree to which particular facts and circumstances may increase risks, compliance procedures, such as due diligence, internal audits, and other appropriate measures, should be correspondingly adjusted to address the heightened risk.

(e) Training and Continuing Advice

In a 'manner appropriate of the targeted audience', pertinent policies and procedures need to be communicated throughout an entity, including to agents, partners, or collaborating entities, whether through training or certifications or other appropriate measures. Measures also must be implemented to ensure that timely advice can be provided to facilitate compliance with an entity's policies.

(f) Incentives and Disciplinary Measures

An entity's compliance programme must be applied throughout an entity. No one should be exempted from its application. Disciplinary procedures must be clear and applied consistently and promptly. Incentives for compliance should be encouraged.

(g) Third-Party Due Diligence and Payments

As part of its 'risk-based' due diligence, the qualifications and associations of third-parties must be understood as well as the business rationale for using the third party. Compliance obligations should be disclosed and commitments obtained from the third parties. Follow-up steps should ensure that the business reasons for using the third party are supported by the terms of any agreements, by the timing and manner in which payments are made, and by there being verification of the work performed. Third-party relationships should be monitored on an on-going basis.

(h) Confidential Reporting and Internal Investigation

A compliance programme should include a mechanism for suspected misconduct to be reported on a confidential basis. Policies should also be implemented to ensure that no one making a confidential disclosure fears retaliation. Adequate resources should be provided so that allegations can be properly investigated and appropriate measures taken.

(i) Continuous Improvement: Periodic Testing and Review

A compliance programme must be regularly tested and reviewed to identify weaknesses, to adjust to changing circumstances and risks and to develop ways of improving its efficiency and effectiveness.

(j) Mergers and Acquisitions: Pre-Acquisition Due Diligence and Post-Acquisition Integration

To avoid legal and business risks, compliance requires that due diligence be performed as part of mergers and acquisitions. The acquired entity should be fully integrated in the internal controls and compliance programme of the acquiring entity. This would extend to all aspects of compliance, such as evaluating and monitoring third parties, training employees and expanding audits to the acquired entity.

b. Civil Sanctions

Civil enforcement actions under the anti-bribery provisions are subject to a civil penalty of $16,000. When the SEC takes action, violations of the anti-bribery provisions are subject to the standard civil enforcement consequences, including injunctions and disgorgement, civil penalty actions involving substantial fines and administrative proceedings. The Justice Department can also seek injunctive relief and the imposition of civil penalties.

c. Collateral Sanctions

An entity that is found to be in violation of the anti-bribery provisions, whether by conviction or the entry of a civil judgment, can be subject to debarment from contracting with the US Government and from seeking various forms of governmental assistance. A suspension or debarment extends to all of the units of an entity. Under some circumstances, suspension of the right to do business with the US Government can take place even before any charges are brought.

In certain situations, misconduct on the part of an officer, director, employee, stockholder or any other individual associated with an entity can be imputed to that same entity for purposes of a debarment. Similarly, in certain circumstances, misconduct on the part of a partner to a joint venture or other joint arrangement may be imputed.

Suspension or disbarment as a result of a violation of the anti-bribery provisions is not limited to a specific programme or agency of a particular country. The suspension or debarment applies to all governmental contracting in the US. In addition, the collateral consequences can be expected to extend to multilateral lending institutions and potentially other governmental agencies in other parts of the world.

As an example, among the provisions of the European Union Public Sector Procurement Directive of 2004 ('EU Procurement Directive') is the requirement that 'any candidate or tenderer' be 'excluded from participation in a public contract' for being the subject of conviction by final judgment of crimes involving corruption, participation in a criminal organisation or money laundering. A conviction for a violation of the anti-bribery provisions may hold the prospect of excluding an individual or entity from participating in public procurements in European Union ('EU') member countries.

B. The Accounting and Record-Keeping Provisions

Unlike the anti-bribery provisions, the FCPA's accounting and record-keeping provisions are not limited to the making of improper inducements to FPOs. They apply to all aspects of an issuer's practices relating to the preparation of its financial statements. The accounting and record-keeping provisions directly affect the worldwide operations of all issuers, including their majority-owned foreign subsidiaries and their officers, directors, employees, shareholders and agents acting on behalf of an issuer. They also directly affect domestic practices, including practices wholly unrelated to the making of improper inducements to FPOs.

The accounting and record-keeping provisions create an affirmative duty on the part of issuers and their officers, directors, employees and agents or stockholders acting on behalf of the issuer. The requirements of what must be proven in order to establish a civil violation are very low. Unlike the anti-bribery provisions, **no proof of intent** is required for civil liability to exist under the accounting and record-keeping provisions. Strict liability is imposed. For a civil violation, all that is required is that the substantive violation be proven by a preponderance of the evidence. This has dramatic ramifications for an issuer.

1. Scope and Application

The scope of the accounting and record-keeping provisions is more limited than the anti-bribery provisions. Specifically, these provisions apply only to issuers. In general, foreign and domestic publicly-held entities that have their shares traded on an exchange in the US are issuers. Although there can be exceptions, issuers can also include foreign entities with ADRs.

a. Subsidiaries of Issuers

Unlike the anti-bribery provisions, the accounting and record-keeping provisions apply directly to the operations of majority-owned foreign subsidiaries of an issuer. However, the accounting and record-keeping provisions are not necessarily applicable to domestic or foreign entities if the issuer holds an interest of 50 per cent or less in the foreign entity.

In addition, in a civil enforcement context, issuers may be held strictly liable for the actions of controlled subsidiaries or foreign affiliates for violations of the accounting and record-keeping provisions. Civil liability may be established without having to prove that an issuer knew or even suspected wrongful conduct on the part of its controlled subsidiary or affiliate.

(1) Less than 50 Per Cent Ownership

When an issuer holds an interest of 50 per cent or less in the foreign entity, the issuer *remains obliged to proceed in good faith* to use its influence to the extent reasonable under the circumstances to cause the affiliated entity to devise and maintain a system of internal controls consistent with the requirements of the accounting and record-keeping provisions. In such circumstances, it will be conclusively presumed to have fulfilled its statutory obligation when it can demonstrate its good faith efforts to influence its subsidiary or affiliate.

(2) Determining Effective Control

In determining whether good faith efforts are exercised, the relevant circumstances include the relative degree of the issuer's ownership of the domestic or foreign firm and the laws and practices governing the business operations of the country in which the subsidiary or affiliate is located. The *degree of effective control* can be expected to bear directly on the evaluation of whether an issuer's efforts are sufficient to demonstrate good faith on its part. An issuer's duty to influence a subsidiary's or affiliate's behaviour increases directly with the degree to which it can exercise control over the subsidiary or affiliate.

b. Individuals

While acting on behalf of an issuer, individuals who are officers, directors, employees, agents or stockholders of an issuer are subject to the terms of the accounting and record-keeping provisions. The scope of the accounting and record-keeping provisions *also* extend to individuals who are officers, directors, employees or agents of a foreign subsidiary where the issuer has an interest greater than 50 per cent.

c. Accomplices

Regardless of whether an individual or entity is subject to the accounting and record-keeping provisions, *any individual or entity can become liable as an accomplice to a violation of the accounting and record-keeping provisions*. This can occur when an individual or entity acts as an aider or abettor to a violation.

(1) Aiders and Abettors

An aider and abettor can be subject to a statutory violation even if that individual or entity cannot be charged directly with violating the statute. Nor is the prosecution of an aider and abettor barred when the principal has been acquitted. To be liable as an aider and abettor, *an individual or entity must act with intent that the offence be committed.*

An individual or entity need not actually violate the accounting and record-keeping provisions. It is the conduct on the part of an individual or entity to **assist** another person's violation that serves as the basis for liability as an accomplice. As a result, an individual or entity not directly subject to the accounting and record-keeping provisions may be exposed to liability as an aider and abettor of an individual or entity subject to the accounting and record-keeping provisions.

(2) Conspirators

Persons not otherwise liable under the accounting and record-keeping provisions can be prosecuted for conspiring to violate their provisions. A conspiracy is established when two or more persons combine or agree to violate a federal statute. If one member takes an act in furtherance of the conspiracy before the other indicates withdrawal from the conspiracy, both can be held criminally liable for having entered into the conspiracy.

When a conspiracy to violate the accounting and record-keeping provisions is involved, no record needs to be falsified and no system of internal controls needs to be circumvented. Nor does it matter that a co-conspirator is a citizen of a foreign country or a foreign entity not normally subject to US law. It is the **agreement** to violate the accounting and record-keeping provisions that serves as the basis for the criminal charge.

The only additional requirement is that there be an overt act by one of the co-conspirators in furtherance of the conspiracy to violate the accounting and record-keeping provisions. Rather insignificant activity can meet this additional requirement.

2. The Record-Keeping Provisions

The record-keeping provisions require an issuer to 'make and keep books, records, and accounts which, in **reasonable detail**, *accurately and fairly reflect the transactions and dispositions* of the assets of the issuer. Reasonable detail is such level of detail and degree of assurance as would satisfy prudent officials in the conduct of their own affairs'.

a. Falsification of Books and Records

An issuer has the responsibility of ensuring that its books and records are accurate so that financial statements can be prepared in conformity with accepted procedures. Falsification of books and records required to be kept under the record-keeping provisions is prohibited. It applies to **any person** and is not limited to officers and directors of an issuer. *The falsification need not be material in terms of the financial statements of an issuer.*

(1) No Requirement for Materiality

The accounting and record-keeping provisions apply to all payments, not merely sums that would be material in the traditional financial sense. Even if the amount of a payment would not affect the 'bottom line' of an issuer in quantitative terms, it could still constitute a violation of the record-keeping provisions if not accurately recorded. As a result of the record-keeping provisions, relatively insignificant amounts of money, if not properly recorded, may have serious ramifications.

(2) Covering Up Misconduct

Although the record-keeping provisions apply to all aspects of the books and records of an issuer, enforcement officials have less tolerance for inaccurate records that may bear on compliance obligations of an issuer. Manipulating books or records to mask transactions by characterizing them in some oblique way, or by actually falsifying a transaction, can lead to serious exposure for an issuer and those individuals involved. For example, placing a transaction into an abnormal category or 'burying' it in some other way may serve as a basis for an enforcement action for a violation of the record-keeping provisions.

In recent years, the SEC's posture has been described as one of 'zero tolerance' for the falsification of records relating to an improper inducement. In other words, the context in which a record may have been falsified, and whether the falsification was an isolated event, will be critical factors in a determination as to whether enforcement action will be taken for a violation of the record-keeping provisions.

Facilitating payments, which are permitted under the anti-bribery provisions, could pose a problem if not accurately described. Similarly, an effort to conceal facilitating payments by placing them among unrelated categories of payments would be improper. A separate line item may not be required as long as the line item in which a facilitating payment is incorporated is both logical and not calculated to conceal.

If, for example, the facilitating payment is a relatively small amount of money and has no relationship to any particular function of an entity, its inclusion in a category of miscellaneous items may not be inappropriate. The degree to which the facilitating payments may be rolled up into larger line items and thereby hidden is not necessarily improper as long as the manner in which such payments are incorporated into a larger line item is logical and not for the purpose of concealing questionable transactions.

(3) Applicable Records

No definitive statement can be made as to what records are subject to the record-keeping provisions. The particular circumstances will ultimately dictate what records are subject to their terms. Generally, the greater the degree to which a record may relate to the preparation of financial statements, the adequacy of internal controls or the performance of audits, the greater the likelihood that the record will be found to be subject to the terms of the record-keeping provisions.

Records such as corporate minutes, transactional documents and authorisations for expenditures are all incidental to the preparation of financial statements or recording economic events. Records that may relate to internal controls, such as compliance programmes, fall within the scope of records subject to the record-keeping provisions since such records bear on the accuracy of the financial statements. Similarly, records that may bear on the auditing of financial statements are likely to be extremely broad in scope and yet subject to the record-keeping provisions.

b. Misrepresentations to Auditors

The record-keeping provisions also prohibit any *officer or director* from making **materially** false or misleading statements or **omitting** to state any **material** facts in the preparation of financial statements. Although this rule applies only to officers and directors, it is very broad in terms of its coverage. *It extends to internal auditors as well as to outside auditors.* It also extends to causing another person to make a material misstatement or make or cause to be made a materially false or misleading statement. Not only are misrepresentations covered, but a material omission or failure to clarify a statement so as not to make it materially false or misleading may constitute a violation.

3. The Internal Controls Provisions

To enhance corporate accountability and ensure that boards of directors, officers and shareholders of issuers are aware of and thus able to prevent the improper use of an issuer's assets, the internal controls provisions require issuers to devise and maintain a system of internal accounting controls sufficient to provide reasonable assurance that:

- transactions are executed in accordance with management's general or specific authorization;
- transactions are recorded as necessary to permit the preparation of financial statements in conformity with generally accepted accounting principles or any other criteria applicable to such statements, and to maintain accountability for assets;
- access to company assets is permitted only in accordance with management's general or specific authorization; and

- the recorded accountability for assets are compared with existing assets at reasonable intervals and appropriate action is taken with respect to any differences.

a. Adequate Internal Controls

The internal controls provisions do not mandate any particular kind of internal controls. The standard for compliance is whether a system, taken as a whole, reasonably meets the statute's objectives. **Reasonable assurance** of management control over an issuer's assets *means such level of detail and degree of assurance as would satisfy prudent officials in the conduct of their own affairs.* The prudent man standard is generally consistent with the expectations of management with respect to their oversight obligations under US law.

Internal controls represent a process designed by an entity's management to provide reasonable assurance regarding the reliability of financial reporting. It has three critical components:

1. Records must be maintained in reasonable detail to accurately and fairly reflect transactions and dispositions of assets;
2. Transactions must be recorded to permit preparation of financial statements in accordance with generally accepted accounting principles, and receipts and expenditures must be properly authorized; *and*
3. Provide reasonable assurance regarding prevention or timely detection of unauthorized acquisition, use or disposition of assets that could have a material effect on an entity's financial statements.

In terms of the third component, steps must be taken to assure compliance with laws and regulations that may have a direct and material effect on the financial statements. Management must assess and adequately address the risk of the entity's vulnerability to events, like 'fraudulent financial reporting, misappropriation of assets, and corruption', that could result in the material misstatement of the entity's financial statements. Adequate internal controls must be implemented to prevent and detect the occurrence of events that may cause or lead to misstatements of financial statements.

'[A] **critical component** of an issuer's internal controls' is an effective compliance programme. The *critical elements* of an effective compliance programme under the internal control provisions are essentially *the same* as those associated with evaluating a compliance programme under the US Sentencing Guidelines relating to violations of the anti-bribery provisions.[1] The same factors may also be determinative as to whether enforcement action may be brought for violations of the internal controls provisions.

An issuer's compliance programme should not necessarily be separate from its system of internal controls. A natural and intended interplay exists between the anti-bribery and the accounting and record-keeping provisions. Indeed, the planning, implementation and monitoring of an issuer's compliance programme should be closely linked, if not intertwined, with its system of internal controls.

b. Broad Reach of the Internal Controls Provisions

The internal controls provisions provide an almost endless series of bases for enforcement action to be taken against an issuer. It must be kept in mind that the internal controls provisions will always be applied in hindsight. When bribery, fraud or other abuses are involved, especially relating to financial transactions, the question will arise as to whether the internal controls were adequate. In such situations, it will be a rare case where the internal controls will be found to be adequate.

Due to their esoteric nature, the internal controls provisions are seldom the focus of criminal enforcement activity. But, in a civil enforcement context, these provisions are frequently used. The standard of proof is a preponderance of the evidence. In almost any after-the-fact analysis relating to financial irregularities, enforcement officials will be able to point to a breakdown of some sort associated with the internal controls of an issuer.

Whether an issuer had knowledge of a defect in its system of internal controls or improperly recorded transactions or other financial activity is irrelevant in the civil enforcement context with respect to the accounting and record-keeping provisions. *No proof of intent is required.*

---

1. The critical elements of an effective compliance programme are described at pages 21-23.

3. Statute of Limitations

The statute of limitations for a criminal or civil violation of the accounting and record-keeping provisions is five years. By agreement, the statute of limitations may be tolled, the equivalent of being placed on hold, for individuals or entities under investigation. In addition, for individuals not resident in the US, the statute of limitations period is also deemed to be tolled for any period the individual is not 'found' within the US where proper service may be made.

4. Sanctions

The standard of proof in a civil enforcement action is a 'preponderance of the evidence' as opposed to the 'beyond a reasonable doubt' standard applicable in a criminal enforcement context. This distinction represents a substantial reduction in the nature and quantum of evidence required to establish a violation of the accounting and record-keeping provisions.

a. Criminal Sanctions

Criminal liability may be established where an individual or entity subject to the accounting and record-keeping provisions knowingly circumvents or fails to implement a system of internal controls or knowingly falsifies any book, record or account.

For criminal liability to be imposed for acts of third parties, an individual or entity must have knowledge that the third party circumvented the internal controls or falsified books and records. Proof of deliberate ignorance or knowing disregard can establish the requisite knowledge, especially when an individual or entity becomes aware of the existence of questionable circumstances.

Criminal violations of the accounting and record-keeping provisions can lead to maximum sentences for an individual of up to twenty years in prison and fines of up to $5 million, or both. Entities can be assessed fines of up to $25 million. Under the alternative sentencing provisions, fines in most situations can be far greater. A fine can be twice the gross gain or, if there is a pecuniary loss to an individual or entity other than the defendant, the fine can be the greater of twice the gross gain or twice the gross loss.

b. Civil Sanctions

Civil enforcement actions under the accounting and record-keeping provisions are subject to a civil penalty of from $7,500 to $150,000 for an individual and $75,000 to $725,000 for an entity. When the SEC takes action, violations of the accounting and record-keeping provisions are subject to the standard civil enforcement consequences including injunctions, which may include disgorgement, civil penalty actions involving substantial fines and administrative proceedings.

c. Collateral Sanctions

An entity that is found to be in violation of the accounting and record-keeping provisions, whether by conviction or the entry of a civil judgment, can be subject to debarment from contracting with the US Government and from seeking various forms of governmental assistance. A suspension or debarment extends to all of the units of an entity. Under some circumstances, suspension of the right to do business with the US Government can take place even before any charges are brought.

In certain situations, misconduct on the part of an officer, director, employee, stockholder or any other individual associated with an entity may be imputed to that entity for purposes of a debarment. Similarly, in certain circumstances, misconduct on the part of a partner to a joint venture or other joint arrangement may be imputed.

C. Other Applicable Laws

1. The Travel Act

A basis also exists under the 'Travel Act' for prosecuting an individual or entity for a violation of what is often referred to as private or commercial bribery. This involves situations where the individual or entity intends to improperly influence someone in the private sector or, in other words, someone who is not a public official. As a result, depending upon the facts of a particular situation, in addition to the bribery of FPOs, individuals and entities may also be held criminally liable for improper inducements in foreign settings to individuals who may not be FPOs.

a. Use of Interstate or Foreign Commerce

Some sort of geographical tie to the US is required for the Travel Act to apply. It must be in the form of travel in interstate or foreign commerce of the US or the use of the mails or any facility of interstate or foreign commerce of the US *in furtherance* of the prohibited conduct. Relatively insignificant activity may be sufficient for the Travel Act to apply. For example, the use of a telephone or email directed to or within the US may be sufficient.

b. Intent and Affirmative Action to Carry on Unlawful Activity

To violate the Travel Act, the travel in or the use of the mails or interstate or foreign commerce must be undertaken with the intent to in some way, whether directly or indirectly, promote or facilitate the unlawful activity. The intent must be accompanied by a sufficient step in furtherance of the unlawful activity that is more than mere preparation. The unlawful activity need not actually take place. An attempt can constitute a violation.

c. Unlawful Activity

For the Travel Act to apply, *there must also be a violation of an underlying state statute prohibiting the unlawful activity.* In the absence of an underlying state statute prohibiting private or commercial bribery, no violation of the Travel Act may occur in the state where the activity in furtherance of the improper inducement took place. For this reason, the scope of application of the Travel Act is more limited than the anti-bribery provisions of the FCPA.

2. Money Laundering

The provisions of the money laundering statutes should always be kept in mind relative to violations of the FCPA. A violation of the FCPA under the anti-bribery and the accounting and record-keeping provisions can serve as a predicate act under the money laundering statutes. A money laundering violation can also have the practical effect of extending the statute of limitations after the expiration of the statute of limitations for the underlying criminal violation.

a. Penalties

Especially in the context of the FCPA's anti-bribery provisions, the term of imprisonment rises from five to twenty years if an individual conducts, or attempts to conduct, a financial transaction with money derived from a violation of the FCPA. The term of imprisonment is ten years if the individual engages in a monetary transaction in criminally derived property. In both instances, alternative fines may be imposed representing twice the value of the amount of the criminally-derived property involved in the transaction.

b. Forfeiture

Any real or personal property constituting or derived from proceeds traceable to a violation of the FCPA, or a conspiracy to violate the FCPA, can be forfeited. The Civil Asset Forfeiture Reform Act of 2000 ('CAFRA') expanded the list of civil forfeiture predicates to include each offense listed as a specified unlawful activity in the Money Laundering Control Act, which includes a violation of the FCPA. CAFRA further provides for criminal forfeiture for all offenses for which civil forfeiture is authorised.

3. Mail and Wire Fraud

In contexts where a scheme or artifice to defraud is involved in combination with the use of interstate or foreign commerce of the US in *furtherance* of the scheme or artifice to defraud, the mail or wire fraud statutes may apply. It does not matter whether the party defrauded is a foreign government or an individual or entity in the private sector. Especially in the context of private or commercial bribery involving kickbacks, a basis for mail or wire fraud charges may exist. Relatively little activity in the U.S. is necessary to establish the use of interstate or foreign commerce.

4. Certification and Reporting Violations

'Certain other licensing, certification, and reporting requirements imposed by the US Government can also be implicated in the foreign bribery context.' For example, as part of securing assistance from the US Government for the export of products, certifications are often required to the effect that an entity has not and will not violate the FCPA, a false certification may result in a criminal violation for a false statement to the US Government.

Along these lines, 'manufacturers, exporters, and brokers of certain defence articles and services are subject to registration, licensing, and reporting requirements under the Arms Export Control Act (AECA) . . . [and] the International Traffic in Arms Regulations (ITAR)'. For manufacturers and exporters of defence articles under AECA and ITAR, 'the sale of defense articles and services valued at $500,000 or more triggers disclosure requirements concerning fees and commissions, including bribes, in an aggregate amount of $100,000 or more'.

5. Tax Violations

Particularly in situations where improper inducements under the FCPA's anti-bribery provisions may have been claimed as a legitimate business expense, violations of US tax law may be involved. Of added significance is the longer six-year statute of limitations that begins to run upon the filing of the tax return in question. The practical effect may be to extend the statute of limitations for a much longer period when a late filing or amended filing of a tax return is involved.

6. Retaliation or Obstructing an Investigation

It is a criminal offence for an individual or entity to knowingly retaliate against any person for providing information relating to the commission or possible commission of a federal offense. *'Retaliation' can consist of 'interfering with the lawful employment or livelihood' of the informant.* An individual could be subject to a term of imprisonment of ten years.

Of added significance is that criminal sanctions can be imposed on an individual or entity for taking action against a whistle blower or anyone seeking to cooperate with a federal investigation. The fact that the individual furnishing the information is located in a foreign setting is not an impediment to prosecution.

In addition, criminal sanctions can be imposed for the destruction, alteration or falsification of records to impede a federal investigation or in anticipation of an investigation and for the destruction of audit records in violation of rules and regulations promulgated by the SEC.

D. Enforcement of the FCPA

1. Enforcement Agencies

The Justice Department is responsible for investigating and prosecuting all criminal charges that are brought against an individual or entity for violations of the FCPA. The SEC cannot bring criminal charges. The SEC's civil enforcement authority is limited to issuers as well as individuals, such as officers, directors, employees, agents and stockholders of issuers and anyone acting on behalf of issuers. All other civil enforcement actions involving the FCPA are left to the Justice Department.[2]

The Justice Department and SEC work together to coordinate their investigations and, to the extent possible, exchange information. Criminal investigations and trials of FCPA cases are conducted by the Justice Department in conjunction with local US Attorneys' offices. Nevertheless, authority to bring criminal charges under the FCPA resides solely with the Justice Department. Even though the Federal Bureau of Investigation ('FBI') has primary responsibility for investigating allegations of FCPA violations, other federal law enforcement agencies can also investigate suspected FCPA violations.

2. Justice Department Enforcement Considerations

In addition to the same factors applicable in determining whether to charge an individual, the Justice Department is required to consider a number of additional factors in determining whether to charge an entity:

- the 'nature and seriousness of the offense', particularly in terms of the risk of harm to the public and applicable policies and priorities relating to certain types of crime;

---

2. Registrants with the Commodities Futures Trading Commission have reporting obligations to the Commission requiring them to report any material noncompliance issues under the Commodities Exchange Act ('Act'), which could include any foreign corrupt practices that may violate the Act.

- the 'pervasiveness of wrongdoing' within the entity and the role of management in participating in or 'condoning' the wrongdoing;
- the entity's 'history of similar misconduct, including prior criminal, civil, and regulatory enforcement actions against it';
- the timeliness of an entity's voluntary disclosure and its willingness to cooperate in the investigation of its agents;
- the 'existence and effectiveness' of the entity's pre-existing compliance programme;
- the entity's 'remedial actions, including any efforts to implement an effective corporate compliance program, to improve an existing one, to replace responsible management, to discipline or terminate wrongdoers, to pay restitution, and to cooperate with the relevant agencies';
- the 'collateral consequences, including whether there is disproportionate harm to shareholders, pension holders, employees, and others not proven personally culpable, as well as impact on the public arising from the prosecution';
- the 'adequacy of the prosecution of individuals responsible' for the entity's misconduct; and
- the 'adequacy of remedies, such as civil or regulatory enforcement actions'.

A number of factors may be inapplicable in some cases and, on occasion, a single factor may be controlling. But generally, no one factor will be determinative. For entities concerned about possible violations, these factors provide guidance as to how best to proceed in addressing the concerns that may arise. For entities that have not adopted a compliance programme or not actively implemented and enforced a compliance programme, these factors should serve to inspire or reinvigorate efforts to ensure that an effective compliance programme is put in place.

One additional factor that must always be kept in mind is the increasing focus of the Justice Department on targeting individuals associated with criminal conduct on the part of entities. In order for an entity to receive credit for co-operation, the Justice Department requires that 'all relevant facts' be provided relating to all individuals responsible for the misconduct, regardless of the level of activity.

3. SEC Enforcement Considerations

A number of factors bear on how allegations concerning a violation may be perceived by the SEC:

- 'Statutes or rules potentially violated';
- 'The egregiousness of the potential violation';
- 'The potential magnitude of the violation';
- 'Whether the potentially harmed group is particularly vulnerable or at risk';
- 'Whether the conduct is ongoing';
- 'Whether the conduct can be investigated efficiently and within the statute of limitations period';
- 'Whether other authorities, including federal or state agencies or regulators, might be better suited to investigate the conduct';
- 'Whether the case involves a possibly widespread industry practice that should be addressed';
- 'Whether the case involves a recidivist'; and
- 'Whether the matter gives the SEC an opportunity to be visible in a community that might not otherwise be familiar with the SEC or the protections afforded by the securities laws'.

4. Deferred-Prosecution and Non-Prosecution Agreements

Increasingly, cases are resolved through deferred-prosecution agreements ('DPA') or non-prosecution agreements ('NPA'). A DPA is filed with the court where the charges are filed. A NPA does not entail the filing of formal charges. Instead, the NPA is maintained by the parties and not filed with the court. DPAs and NPAs represent a 'middle ground' between the Justice Department declining prosecution and bringing charges against an entity.

The conditions associated with DPAs and NPAs can be expected to be onerous and costly for an entity. The level and nature of cooperation and factors such as voluntary disclosure and disgorgement will be among the critical considerations of the Justice Department. The SEC requires that there be a voluntary disclosure for DPAs and NPAs to be even considered.

Yet by entering into a DPA or NPA, an entity limits its exposure and brings to an end the disruptions and uncertainties associated with an investigation. Such a step may also enhance an entity's chances of reaching a global resolution that may avoid debarment and other adverse consequences associated with entering a plea or being subject to drawn-out criminal proceedings.

In most instances, a failure to abide by a DPA or a NPA allows the Justice Department, in its sole discretion, to file charges against the entity. By entering into the agreement, an entity, in effect, admits to the charges. As a result, the Justice Department does not have to go to trial to prove the charges at a later point in time.

5. Monitors

Many DPAs or NPAs require an independent monitor to be retained. The factors that are considered in determining the need for a monitor include:

- 'Seriousness of the offense';
- 'Duration of the misconduct';
- 'Pervasiveness of the misconduct, including whether the conduct cuts across geographic and/or product lines';
- 'Nature and size of the company';
- 'Quality of the company's compliance program at the time of the misconduct'; and
- 'Subsequent remediation efforts'.

A monitor's primary responsibility is to assess and monitor an entity's compliance with the terms of the DPA or NPA. It is not to further 'punitive goals'. A monitor's duties are to be no broader than necessary and should be tailored to the particular situation. Particularly where an entity has made a 'voluntary disclosure', 'been fully cooperative' and 'demonstrated genuine commitment to reform, self-monitoring may be permitted'.

6. Independent Compliance Consultants

Among the remedies imposed by the SEC as part of a resolution is the requirement that an entity retain an independent compliance consultant ('ICC') acceptable to the SEC to review and evaluate an entity's policies and procedures relating to its internal controls, record-keeping and financial reporting relating to compliance with the anti-bribery and accounting and record-keeping provisions of the FCPA. The entity must bear the full cost of the ICC's fees and expenses.

Chapter 3
UK Bribery Act

For many years, the UK law on bribery was to be found in a number of sources but chiefly in the Public Bodies Corrupt Practices Act of 1889 and the Prevention of Corruption Acts of 1906 and 1916. In 1999 the OECD Convention on Combating Bribery of Foreign Public Officials ('OECD Anti-Bribery Convention') required its signatories, which included the UK, to establish in their national laws a criminal offence of bribing a foreign public official. Subsequently, the UK was criticised by the OECD for being slow to respond and was urged to adopt appropriate legislation as a matter of priority.

The UK responded by drawing up a Bribery Bill, which was placed before Parliament and provided the foundation for the UK Bribery Act. The UK Bribery Act came into force on 1 July 2011. Its provisions are not retrospective, which means that it applies to acts of bribery committed after that date. The UK Bribery Act consolidates the law in a single source, abolishes the common law offences and repeals former statutory offences. However, the old law remains in force with regard to offences of bribery committed wholly or partly *prior* to 1 July 2011.

A. The General Offences

The provisions of the UK Bribery Act are of general application to bribery within the *public and private sectors*.[3] The general offences under the UK

---

3. This differs from the FCPA whose anti-bribery provisions are directed at FPOs and do not have a general application.

Bribery Act, sections 1, 2 and 3 ('General Offences') apply to bribery where any act or omission forming part of the offence takes place *within the UK*. Where bribery takes place *outside the UK*, the courts of the UK have jurisdiction under sections 1, 2 or 6 if:

- The acts or omissions would form part of the offence if done or made in the UK, and
- The person concerned had a **'close connection'** with the UK, which will include a foreign citizen ordinarily resident in the UK.

1. Bribing another Person ('Active Bribery') – Section 1

This occurs where a financial or other advantage is offered, promised or given to individuals or entities with the intention of inducing or rewarding the improper performance of a relevant function or activity.

- *'Relevant function or activity'* means any function of a public nature, or any activity that is connected with a business or performed in the course of a person's employment or performed by or on behalf of a body of persons.
- *'Improper performance'* may take place where the relevant function is performed in breach of an *expectation* that it is performed in good faith, impartially and in accordance with a position of trust.
- *'Expectation test'* is what a reasonable person in the UK would expect in relation to the performance of the type of function or activity concerned.

2. Being Bribed ('Passive Bribery') – Section 2

This occurs where a financial or other advantage is requested or accepted in return for the improper performance of a relevant function or activity.[4] The same considerations as in section 1 apply as to what is improper

---

4. The UK Bribery Act differs from the FCPA, which does not cover Passive Bribery. However, in rare situations, money laundering has served as the basis of a criminal charge by the US Justice Department for conduct that might otherwise be described as Passive Bribery.

performance or relevant function or activity. Section 2 differs in that it focuses on those who seek or receive the financial or other advantage.

3. Bribing a Foreign Public Official ('FPO') – Section 6

This occurs where a financial or other advantage is offered, promised or given to a foreign public official, or to another person at the FPO's request or with their acquiescence, *with intent:*

- to influence that person in their capacity as an FPO; and
- to obtain or retain business or a business advantage.[5]

a. Foreign Public Official
An *FPO* is an individual who:

(i)   holds a *legislative, administrative* or *judicial position* of any kind, whether appointed or elected, of a country or territory outside the UK;

(ii)   exercises a *public function* on behalf of a country or territory outside the UK;[6] or

(iii) is an official or agent of a *public international organisation.*[7]

A 'public function' will include individuals and entities who perform public functions in any branch of national, local or municipal government. It will also embrace those who exercise a public function for a public agency or enterprise, such as professionals working for public health agencies and officers exercising public functions in state-owned enterprises. A 'public

---

5. The threshold for a violation for an improper inducement to an FPO under the UK Bribery Act is lower than that under the FCPA. No proof of corrupt intent is required for an improper inducement to an FPO to be a violation under the UK Bribery Act.

6. The definition of what constitutes an FPO under the FCPA is somewhat broader than that under the UK Bribery Act. In particular, political parties, officials of political parties and candidates for office are included under the FCPA.

7. Whereas the UK Bribery Act relies upon a broad definition, the FCPA relies upon a list of international organisations that have been specifically designated by the US Government as being subject to diplomatic immunity.

international organisation' will include people who work for example for organisations such as the UN or the World Bank.

b. Interaction between Sections 1 and 6

Particular conduct may constitute a bribery offence under both section 1 and section 6. The UK Government policy behind the FPO offence in section 6 is the need to prohibit the influencing of decision making in the context of publicly funded business opportunities by the inducement of personal enrichment of FPOs.

To be required to rely solely on section 1 for this would require proof of 'improper performance' of a relevant function, something which, in the case of an FPO, is often difficult accurately to establish. For this reason, the 'standalone' offence under section 6 does not contain the 'improper performance' requirement contained in section 1.

4. Liability of a Corporation for a General Offence

Under UK law, an entity will have imputed to it the acts and state of mind of those of its directors and managers who represent its *directing mind and will*.[8] Accordingly, an entity may be exposed to prosecution under sections 1, 2 or 6 if a person in a sufficiently senior position commits bribery on behalf of the entity under any of those sections.

5. Exceptions, Affirmative Defences and Related Considerations

Depending on the circumstances, the UK Bribery Act may not be applicable or enforced in every situation.

a. Statutory Limitations

The UK does not have an equivalent to the US statute of limitations. The position in the UK is that, unless otherwise provided by statute, there is no time limit within which a prosecution must be brought. For example, the Magistrates' Courts Act 1980 provides that *summary* proceedings must, in general, be commenced within six months of the commission of the offence.

---

8. A more complete explanation is provided on page 56 under subpart 3.

b. Relevance of a Country's Written Law

The section 6 offence is not committed where the official is permitted or required by the *written* law of the country concerned to be influenced by the advantage. This might occur, for example, where the local written law permits an official to be influenced in circumstances where those tendering for publicly funded contracts offer some form of investment that will be of benefit to the local community.

The mere fact that a particular payment is in accordance with *local custom* will not afford a defence.

6. The UK Enforcement Approach to *Business Expenditure*

The UK Bribery Act makes no specific provision for reasonable and *bona fide* business expenditure. The UK Government, however, has made it clear that nothing in the UK Bribery Act is intended to criminalise *bona fide* hospitality or other business expenditure which seeks to improve the image of an entity, to better present products and services, or to establish cordial relations, recognising that these things are an established and important part of doing business.

a. Need for Caution

This is, however, a risk area for entities. Unless care is taken, there may in a particular case be an irresistible inference from the facts that that the real purpose behind the expenditure in question was to influence the recipient to secure business or a business advantage in circumstances which amounted to a bribe under the UK Bribery Act.

b. Basic Safeguards

Much in this area is a matter of common sense, but the following steps may be taken by an entity to protect itself from adverse exposure to the UK Bribery Act:

1. having a specific *policy* on its approach to business expenditure, if necessary setting limits and defining the circumstances in which prior approval at a high level of the entity may be required;

2. articulating in writing the *procedure* to be followed by employees incurring business expenditure;
3. ensuring, where applicable, that such expenditure is *permitted under local law*; and
4. maintaining *registers* of the entity which record each and every occasion upon which such expenditure occurs.

c. Proportionality

Each case will depend upon its surrounding circumstances but in the final analysis the crucial consideration will be whether the expenditure concerned was reasonable and proportionate.

Levels of expenditure will of course be a major determining feature here. The more lavish the hospitality or the higher the expenditure in relation to travel, accommodation or other similar business expenditure, the easier the inference may be that it was intended to obtain business or a business advantage in return, and therefore to constitute a bribe.

This factor was recognised in the Guidance for Commercial Organisations ('Government Guidance') issued by the Secretary of State under the UK Bribery Act.

But also relevant will be matters such as the nature of the expenditure relative to the recipient's position, the frequency of such expenditure on the entity in question, its timing and whether it is commensurate with the norms in a particular sector.

d. The Approach of the UK Serious Fraud Office ('SFO')

In October 2012 the UK Serious Fraud Office ('SFO') issued a revised statement of policy regarding business expenditure in which it:

- reaffirmed that 'bona fide' hospitality or promotional or other legitimate business expenditure is recognised as an established and important part of doing business;
- indicated that it would prosecute offenders who disguised bribes as business expenditure; but only if:
    a. it was a serious or complex case falling within the SFO's remit *and*, if so,

b. the SFO concluded, applying the Full Code Test in the Code
    for Crown Prosecutors, that there was an offender that should
    be prosecuted.

The 'Full Code Test' requires the prosecutor to be satisfied, first, that there
is *sufficient evidence* to provide a realistic prospect of conviction and, sec-
ondly, that a prosecution is required in the *public interest*.

7. The UK Enforcement Approach to *Facilitating Payments*

Facilitating payments are usually small payments made to expedite or to
secure the performance of a routine governmental action by an FPO. They
relate essentially to non-discretionary acts by FPOs and include such things
as payments to obtain official documents or to receive services.[9]

a. The OECD Approach

In 2009 the OECD asked countries which are signatories to the OECD
Anti-Bribery Convention to *discourage* the making of such payments, recognising the corrosive effect of such payments. The UK Bribery Act does not
provide any form of exception for such payments and they remain illegal.

The UK Government's approach to this subject is that exemptions in this
context create artificial distinctions that are difficult to enforce, undermine
an entity's anti-bribery procedures, confuse anti-bribery communications
with employees and other associated persons, perpetuate an existing 'culture' of bribery and have the potential to be abused.

b. The Need for Caution

The making of such payments has the potential for constituting offences
under section 1 and section 6 of the UK Bribery Act and consequentially for
entities under section 7. There is, therefore, a need for caution in this area.

The Government Guidance recognises the problems that commercial
organisations face in some parts of the world and in certain sectors and
suggests that businesses have a role to play in the long-term eradication of

---

9. The contrasting US position on facilitating payments is that, through an exception, they
are permitted under the FCPA.

such payments by means of bribery prevention procedures which address this subject.

It is also recognised that there are occasions when such demands are accompanied by threats to life, limb or liberty. In such instances, it is almost inconceivable that the SFO would take action and in any event the common law defence of duress would probably be available.

Because the UK does not sanction such payments, entities need to have some guidance on how to instruct those of their employees who may be asked to make them.

c. Basic Safeguards

In order to protect themselves from potential exposure to the UK Bribery Act and as a matter of good business practice, it is suggested that an entity might be advised to have the following basic systems in place:

1. A defined policy committing the entity to the avoidance, where possible, of facilitating payments.
2. Written communication of this policy to its staff and it agents.
3. A clearly defined and widely communicated procedure to be followed by members of staff, when asked to make such payments. Such a procedure might include questioning the legitimacy of the demand, requesting to speak to the FPO's superior, asking for a receipt and identification details of the officials concerned and reporting to the entity every occasion when such a payment is made.
4. Training of relevant staff on this procedure.
5. For its part an entity should:
   - maintain a careful written record of the occasions when such payments are made, the sums involved and confirmation that the employees concerned had followed the defined procedure before making the payments; and
   - make use, wherever possible, of diplomatic channels and sectoral organisations to put pressure on the authorities in the countries concerned to take action regarding such demands.

d. The Approach of the SFO to Facilitating Payments

In October 2012 the SFO issued a revised statement of policy regarding facilitating payments in which it:

- affirmed that facilitating payments remained illegal following the UK Bribery Act; and
- indicated that prosecution in these cases would depend upon:

  (a) whether it was a serious or complex case falling within the SFO's remit and, if so,
  (b) whether the SFO concluded, applying the Full Code Test, that there was an offender that should be prosecuted.

In December 2012, the Director of the SFO issued an 'open letter' in which he made the following points:

1. that facilitation payments are illegal under the UK Bribery Act regardless of their size or frequency;
2. that UK individuals or companies asked to make such payments in the course of doing business overseas should inform the Foreign and Commonwealth Office via the local embassy, high commission or consulate;
3. that the SFO might communicate such information to a law enforcement agency in the country where the request was made; and
4. that the SFO is ready to take effective action against the use of facilitating payments, regardless of where they are requested.

Thus there seems to be a clear message from the SFO that enforcement of the law which forbids the making of facilitating payments is already a significant item on its agenda.

8. Political Contributions

There is no bar in the UK to the making of political contributions, lobbying or awarding directorships or consultancies to politicians.

This is, however, an area of potential risk for entities, because the circumstances may be such as to give rise to an overwhelming inference that the action was designed to provide the entity with business or a business advantage in exchange. The risk of such an inference is particularly acute where a political contribution is made in a country outside the UK. If this is envisaged, it should first be established that such a contribution is legal in the country concerned

Because of these sensitivities, some entities prohibit the making of political contributions. Where, however, entities are inclined to make them, it is suggested that safeguards such as the following are put in place:

- A clear and publicly accessible statement of an entity's policy on these matters;
- A defined entity procedure for considering and giving approval to such proposals; and
- A readily accessible record of any political contribution.

9. Charitable Donations

An entity may legitimately make contributions to charities and undertake sponsorships. However this is also a risk area because of the possibility of such funds being used as a cover for bribery or the making of kickbacks. If this should occur, an entity may find itself criminally liable.

Particular caution is required where the contribution is to be made outside the UK. In some countries, entities wishing to do business or obtain licences have been invited to contribute to projects which will be of benefit to the local community.

If an entity's genuine motivation is to assist the local community, then the contribution will be legitimate. If the real motivation is to influence business or to reward a contract award, then this will be bribery.

Entities inclined to make such contributions should consider the following safeguards:

- A policy covering its approach to charitable contributions;
- A clear and accessible record of all such contributions;

- Full due diligence on the structure, personnel and financial standing of the charity concerned and of any third party through whom the payment is to be made;
- No payments to be made in cash; and
- Monitoring payments to ensure that they reach the intended recipients.

10. Sanctions for General Offences

An *individual* found guilty of any of the General Offences under sections 1, 2 and 6 will be liable to imprisonment for up to ten years or to an unlimited fine or to both. An *entity* found guilty of any of the General Offences will be liable to an unlimited fine. Definitive guidelines on sentencing in such cases became effective in October 2014.

Additionally, an *entity* convicted of an offence under section 1 or section 2 will face *mandatory debarment* from tendering for government contracts under the EU Procurement Directive.

B. Liability of Senior Officers

Under section 14, where it can be demonstrated that an offence under sections 1, 2 or 6 has been committed by a body corporate, a **senior officer** who is proved to have **consented to** or **connived in** the offence will be guilty of the same offence and liable to imprisonment for up to ten years or to a fine or to both.

In order, however, to be liable for this offence the senior officer concerned must have a **'close connection'** with the UK, and this would include a foreign citizen ordinarily resident in the UK. The term 'senior officer' means a director, manager, secretary or other similar officer of a body corporate.

C. The Corporate Offence – Failure to Prevent Bribery

The UK Bribery Act creates in section 7 an offence applicable only to commercial entities, namely that of Failure of Commercial Organisations to Prevent Bribery.[10]

This offence is committed by a *relevant commercial organisation* where a *person associated with it* commits the general offence of 'Active Bribery' or of bribing an FPO, *intending* to obtain business or an advantage in the conduct of business for the entity.

This is an extremely far-reaching provision because:

- this offence applies to bribery in both the public and the private sectors;
- there is no requirement that an individual who commits the bribery should be a UK national or even resident in the UK; and
- it is not a requirement that any of the acts of bribery should have taken place in the UK.

1. Relevant Commercial Organisations

The corporate offence applies only to a 'relevant commercial organisation'. Such an entity is defined in the UK Bribery Act as being a corporate body or a partnership, *wherever in the world incorporated or formed*, which **carries on a business** or part of a business in the UK.

The scope of this description has already been much discussed and awaits judicial scrutiny. However, the Government Guidance advocates a 'common sense approach' and suggests that entities from *outside* the UK would need to have a 'demonstrable business presence' in the UK in order to be liable.

---

10. The FCPA does not contain a provision equivalent to the section 7 offence. Yet, from a conceptual standpoint, similarities exist in the manner in which the adequacy of a compliance programme is taken into account by US officials in determining whether to bring an enforcement action for an FCPA violation.

a. Parents and Subsidiaries

The Government Guidance points out that having a subsidiary in the UK will not in itself mean that an overseas parent entity is necessarily carrying on a business in the UK. It is established law that the liabilities of a subsidiary are not those of the parent. This is known as the 'corporate veil' principle. However, this veil may be pierced, depending on the particular facts of a case.

Overseas parent entities need to examine carefully whether the facts are such that the only reasonable interpretation is that the parent is *in fact* carrying on a business in the UK through the activities of its subsidiary, so as to make the parent potentially liable under section 7 of the Act.

The fact that an overseas entity may own or have a considerable stake in a UK entity or that a number of its directors may sit on the board will not necessarily pierce the corporate veil. Nor will economic links between the two entities. If, however, the evidence indicates that the corporate structure is designed in such a way as to defeat potential exposure of the parent to the UK Bribery Act, then the corporate veil will be pierced.

b. Organisations Pursuing Charitable or Similar Aims

It is made clear in the Government Guidance and important to note that an incorporated organisation or partnership which pursues primarily charitable or educational aims or purely public functions will be potentially subject to the UK Bribery Act, if it engages in commercial activities, irrespective of the purpose for which profits are made.

c. The Need for Caution

This offence, because of its wide application, needs therefore to be taken very seriously by any overseas entity which has a business 'footprint' in the UK.

2. Associated Persons

A 'relevant commercial organisation' only becomes exposed to this offence if a **person associated with it** commits bribery **intending to obtain or retain business** for the entity.

The UK Bribery Act defines an associated person as being one who **performs services** for or on behalf of the entity. Whether or not this is the case has to be determined by reference to all the relevant circumstances. Three instances are quoted in the UK Bribery Act by way of example, namely employees, agents and subsidiaries.

Government Guidance, however, emphasises that the concept of a person performing services for or on behalf of an entity is intended to give the section 7 corporate offence *broad scope*, so as to embrace 'the whole range of persons connected to an organisation who might be capable of committing bribery on the organisation's behalf'. So this concept may apply to an entity's contractors, its suppliers or its joint venture partners.

The scope of the concept has also provoked much debate and will require judicial examination. However, the courts might be expected to adopt a broad interpretative approach, in order to follow the legislature's clear intention in this regard.

3. The 'Absolute' Nature of the Corporate Offence

Under what is known as the 'Identification Doctrine', an entity in the UK will have imputed to it the acts and state of mind of those of its directors and managers who represent its 'directing mind and will'.[11] With regard to the General Offences under sections 1, 2 and 6, for an entity to be liable it will still be necessary to prove that the offence was committed by a person representing the 'directing mind and will' of the entity.[12]

However, the Identification Doctrine does not preclude the legislature from prohibiting an act or enforcing a duty in words which make the prohibition or the duty *absolute*. This is precisely what has happened with regard to the offence of Failure of Commercial Organisations to Prevent Bribery. The words of section 7 make it clear that there is no requirement to prove that anyone at board or senior management level either participated in or even knew of the bribery.

---

11. The general principle at Common Law is that a master is not to be made criminally responsible for those acts of his servants to which the master is not a party. However, the question was considered in Tesco Supermarkets Ltd. v Nattrass [1972] AC 153, which led to the Identification Doctrine.

12. The Identification Doctrine differs from US law where it is the sum of knowledge of an entity's officers, directors, employees and agents, when acting within the scope of their employment or responsibilities, that establishes knowledge on behalf of an entity.

4. The 'Adequate Procedures' Defence

The UK Bribery Act provides a statutory defence if the entity can prove (on a balance of probabilities) that when the bribery occurred, it had in place 'adequate procedures' designed to prevent associated persons from undertaking such conduct. It is a requirement of the UK Bribery Act that the Secretary of State publish Government Guidance about procedures that relevant commercial entities can put in place to prevent associated persons from bribing.

The Government Guidance is not binding but may be regarded as a useful template, against which an organisation can measure its anti-bribery procedures. The principles are 'intended to be flexible . . . allowing for the huge variety of circumstances that commercial organisations find themselves in'. It is suggested that bribery prevention procedures should be proportionate to risk.

The UK Bribery Act allows for revisions to the Government Guidance to be published from time to time. The Government Guidance published in March 2011 is based upon six principles as follows:

(a) Proportionate Procedures
'A commercial organisation's procedures to prevent bribery by persons associated with it are proportionate to the bribery risk it faces and to the nature, scale and complexity of the commercial organisation's activities. They are also clear, practical, accessible, effectively implemented and enforced'.

(b) Top-Level Commitment
'The top-level management of a commercial organisation (be it a board of directors, the owners or any equivalent body or person) are committed to preventing bribery by persons associated with it. They foster a culture within the organisation in which bribery is never acceptable'.

(c) Risk Assessment
'The commercial organisation assesses the nature and extent of its exposure to potential external and internal risks of bribery on its behalf by persons associated with it. The assessment is periodic, informed and documented'.

(d) Due Diligence

'The commercial organisation applies due diligence procedures, taking a proportionate and risk-based approach, in respect of persons who perform or will perform services for or on behalf of the organisation, in order to mitigate identified bribery risks'.

(e) Communication (including training)

'The commercial organisation seeks to ensure that its bribery prevention policies and procedures are embedded and understood throughout the organisation through internal and external communication, including training, that is proportionate to the risk it faces'.

(f) Monitoring and Review

'The commercial organisation monitors and reviews procedures designed to prevent bribery by persons associated with it and makes improvements where necessary'.

5. Sanctions for the Corporate Offence

An entity convicted of this offence may be subject to an unlimited fine and orders for compensation and confiscation. Definitive guidelines on sentencing in such cases became effective in October 2014.

Additionally, an entity convicted of an offence under section 7 may face debarment for up to five years from participation in public contractual work within the EU.

D. Other Applicable Laws

1. Bribery and Money Laundering – The Proceeds of Crime Act ('POCA')

The connection between the receipt of bribes and money laundering is obvious. It will often be the case that the recipient of a bribe will make a significant attempt to transfer or conceal such ill-gotten gains. Where there is evidence of this, the SFO may consider money laundering in the form of an additional charge.

The principal legislation on this subject is contained in the Proceeds of Crime Act 2002 ('POCA').

The POCA includes the following principal offences:

(a) Concealing, disguising, converting, transferring, removing, acquiring, using or having possession of **criminal property**. ('Criminal property' is that which constitutes or represents a person's benefit from criminal conduct and where the alleged offender knows or suspects that to be the case.)

(b) Entering into or becoming concerned in an *arrangement* knowing or suspecting that it *facilitates the acquisition* or control of criminal property by or on behalf of another person and knowing that it constitutes or represents such benefit.

The offences set out in paragraphs (a) and (b) above carry a *penalty* of up to fourteen years imprisonment or a fine or both.

(c) *Failing to disclose* possible money laundering.

   i.   Failure by a *person working in the regulated sector* to disclose to a nominated officer information whereby he knows or suspects or has reasonable grounds for knowing or suspecting that another person is engaged in money laundering. (The 'regulated sector' broadly speaking covers credit and financial institutions and also activities undertaken by different categories of professional advisers, such as auditors, accountants, tax advisers, insolvency practitioners and independent legal professionals.)

   ii. Failure by a *nominated officer* in the regulated sector, receiving a report of known or suspected money laundering to disclose such report to an authorised person as soon as practicable.

   iii. Failure by a *nominated officer*, whether inside or outside the regulated sector, to disclose to an authorised person as soon as practicable a report coming to the discloser in the course of a trade, profession, business or employment.

   These 'failing to disclose' provisions carry a penalty of up to five years imprisonment or a fine or both.

(d) Tipping off

   An offence is committed where a person, in the course of business in the regulated sector, discloses to a customer or other person that a money laundering investigation is being contemplated or carried out and where such disclosure is likely to be prejudicial.

This offence carries a penalty of up to two years imprisonment or a fine or both.

2. Accounting and Bookkeeping

The UK Bribery Act contains no provisions which correspond with the accounting and record-keeping provisions of the FCPA. However, two pieces of UK legislation may be of relevance in this context:

a. False Accounting under the Theft Act 1968

Under section 17 it is a criminal offence dishonestly and with a view to gain to falsify an account or record required for an accounting purpose. Thus, an offence under this section would be committed by an entity's employee who 'doctored' accounting records in order to cover up a bribe payment.

b. Failing to Keep Accounting Records under the Companies Act 2006

If an entity fails in its duty to keep adequate accounting records, an offence is committed under section 387 by every officer of the entity who is in default. This form of 'unlawful conduct' has been used by the SFO as the basis for the obtaining of Civil Recovery Orders ('CRO').

3. Company Directors Disqualification

Sections 1 and 2 of the Company Directors Disqualification Act 1986 enable a court to make an order disqualifying a director convicted of an indictable offence in connection with an entity for a specified period of up to fifteen years.

4. Aiders and Abettors

Those who assist a principal offender in carrying out an offence of bribery are regarded as 'Aiders and Abettors', while those who encourage the commission of an offence are classified as 'Counsellors and Procurers'.

For liability to attach as a secondary party, it is necessary for that party to know of the matters essential to the principal offence and to have the intention of assisting or encouraging the principal offender in what they are doing.

Thus, where an employee commits bribery to the knowledge of his manager and the manager chooses to take no action, liability may attach to the manager as a secondary party.

5. Conspirators

The essence of a criminal conspiracy lies in the agreement. Nothing need be done in pursuit of such agreement for the offence to be complete.

a. Statutory Offence of Conspiracy

This applies to a situation in which two or more persons agree to pursue a course of conduct which, if carried out in accordance with their intentions, will involve the commission of an offence.

Thus, if at least two persons agree to offer a bribe, they will be liable to prosecution for conspiring to contravene the provisions of section 1 of the UK Bribery Act.

b. Conspiracy to Defraud

The common law offence of conspiracy to defraud is committed where two or more persons agree to pursue a course that is intended to prejudice or take the risk of prejudicing another's right.

E. Enforcement of the UK Bribery Act

1. Enforcement Agencies

Proceedings under the UK Bribery Act may be instituted by the Director of Public Prosecutions, the Director of the Serious Fraud Office or the Director of Revenue and Customs Prosecutions. In practice, however, the Director of the SFO bears primary responsibility for enforcing the UK Bribery Act.

2. Acceptance of Cases

The SFO does not accept for investigation every case which is referred to it, nor is it resourced to do so. It receives an annual grant from the Treasury, which has been steadily decreasing. In exceptional cases, the Treasury may provide the SFO with special 'blockbuster' funding.

In deciding whether or not to accept a case, the SFO relies upon a number of criteria, which include the nature and complexity of the matter, the degree of public interest in it and whether the case has an international dimension. At the conclusion of an investigation, the SFO has three alternative choices: (1) take no further action; (2) commence criminal proceedings, or (3) obtain a Civil Recovery Order.

3. Criminal Proceedings

This course will only be pursued if:

(a) the evidence discloses a *reasonable prospect of conviction* (the 'evidential test'), and

(b) it is in the *public interest* for the case to be prosecuted (the 'public interest test').

4. Deferred Prosecution Agreements ('DPAs')

In February 2014, legislation came into force enabling the Director of the SFO or the Director of Public Prosecutions to enter into a DPA with a company, partnership or unincorporated association in certain cases of financial crime, including bribery.

Pursuant to legislative requirements, the SFO and the Crown Prosecution Service published a Code of Conduct to be followed by prosecutors when negotiating DPAs, when applying to the court for approval of a DPA or when overseeing DPAs following such approval.

The prescribed procedure involves a number of sequential steps:

1. The prosecutor will apply a *two-stage test* to determine (a) whether the available evidence establishes a realistic prospect of conviction and, if so, (b)whether the public interest would be properly served by not prosecuting.

2. If this test be satisfied, the prosecutor may initiate negotiations by sending a *Letter of Invitation* to the entity concerned.

3. Negotiations may then commence and in due course the prosecutor will apply to the Crown Court for a *Preliminary Hearing*, held in private, at which a judge will be asked to make a declaration that a DPA would be in the interests of justice and that the proposed terms are fair, reasonable and proportionate.
4. Following such approval, the prosecutor and the entity will finalise the Agreement and a *Final Hearing* will take place in open court, at which the judge will make a declaration approving the DPA and giving reasons for so doing.
5. Following the Final Hearing, the prosecutor is required to publish on its website the DPA and the declarations of the court at the Initial and Private Hearings.[13]

Breach of a DPA may lead to a court order that it be terminated and a prosecution of the entity concerned may then ensue.

5. Civil Recovery Order ('CRO')

The POCA allows enforcement authorities to recover, in civil proceedings before the High Court, property which is, or represents, property obtained through '*unlawful conduct*'. Should the SFO determine that a civil settlement is appropriate, it will seek to include in the CRO matters such as the following:

(a) a *financial penalty*, which will reflect the sums received from the conduct and might include interest and the SFO's costs;
(b) *monitoring* by an independent and well-qualified individual, nominated by the entity and acceptable to the SFO, to review enhanced compliance procedures intended to reduce the risk of the unlawful conduct recurring;

---

13. The first application of this new procedure was concluded in November 2015 when the court approved an application by the SFO for a DPA in a case where the counter-party, *Standard Bank PLC*, was the subject of an indictment alleging failure to prevent bribery contrary to section 7 of the UK Bribery Act. This was followed by four more cases involving the approval of DPAs, namely *XYZ* (July 2016), *Rolls Royce* (January 2017), *Tesco Stores Limited* (January 2019) and *Serco Geografix Limited* (July 2019).

(c) an agreed programme of *culture change and training*; and

(d) discussion regarding *the position of individuals*.

Should the terms of a civil settlement be agreed, a joint public statement will be required in the interests of transparency.[14]

An advantage of such a negotiated settlement over a criminal prosecution is that the mandatory debarment provisions under the EU Procurement Directive will not apply to a negotiated settlement.

6. Principles Determining the SFO's Course of Action

In determining which course to pursue in any individual case, the SFO will consider all the surrounding circumstances and the following matters in particular are likely to play a significant part in such a decision, namely:

(a) whether the entity, having itself become aware of the unlawful conduct, had **self-referred** the matter to the SFO,

(b) the degree of co-operation afforded by the entity following a self-report, which will include identifying relevant witnesses, making them available for interviews when requested, disclosing relevant accounts and documents and providing a report in respect of any internal investigation,

(c) whether what had occurred was not systemic but was simply an **isolated incident**, which had slipped through the net of an otherwise adequate anti-bribery procedural system,

(d) a lack of history of similar conduct, and

(e) efforts by the entity to improve its anti-bribery procedures.

7. Self-Referral

a. SFO Policy

In October 2012, the SFO issued a revised statement of policy on corporate self-reporting. It emphasised that for a self-report to be taken into account

---

14. A good example of such a statement is to be found in the press release, which followed the SFO's settlement in July 2012 with Oxford Publishing Ltd, in which the company agreed to pay almost £1.9 million after admitting unlawful conduct in its East African operations.

as a public interest factor against prosecution 'it must form part of a *genuinely proactive approach* adopted by the corporate management team'. It also pointed out that failure to report properly and fully the *true extent* of the wrongdoing or *within a reasonable time* of it coming to light would be public interest factors in favour of a prosecution.

The revised policy stipulates that self-reporting will be no guarantee that a prosecution will not follow and that each case will turn on its own facts. The proper approach to be adopted by entities and/or their advisers when self-reporting to the SFO is set out as follows:

- *Initial contact* and all subsequent communication must be made through the SFO's Intelligence Unit 3.[15]
- *Hard copy reports* setting out the nature and scope of any internal investigation must be provided to the SFO's Intelligence Unit as part of the self-reporting process.
- All *supporting evidence* including, but not limited to, banking evidence and witness accounts, must be provided to the SFO's Intelligence Unit as part of the self-reporting process.

b. The Decision Whether or Not to Self-Report

In the UK there is no overriding duty for an entity to self-refer discovered wrongdoing to the authorities and it is recognised that a decision whether to approach the SFO may not be an easy one for a corporate.

The SFO would not expect to be informed about every matter which an entity might uncover in this regard. If the matter were not systemic and of a nature which an entity might properly deal with through its own internal disciplinary and other procedures, then there would be arguable grounds for not self-referring. If, however, the matter were of such a nature that on any reasonable view it needed to be drawn to the attention of the SFO, then there should be a self-referral.

c. Specific Guidance to Corporates

There is no system in the UK akin to the FCPA Opinion Procedure.

---

15. The relevant email address is confidential@sfo.gsi.gov.uk.

In the past, the SFO was occasionally amenable to giving guidance when entities faced with a particular or potential problem sought its advice.

In reviewing its policy on facilitating payments, business expenditure and self-reporting by entities, the SFO has emphasised that it is primarily an investigator and prosecutor of serious fraud and corruption and that it is not its role to provide entities with advice on their future conduct.

8. The Current Direction

The SFO has been keen to stress that it intends in the future to focus on cases:

(a) which compromise a proper 'level playing field' in business;
(b) where serious national or international bribery and corruption are concerned;
(c) which have a strong public interest element; or
(d) which involve some new species of fraud.

All the indications are that the SFO will have a greater appetite than in the recent past to pursue through the criminal courts those cases which satisfy the evidential and the public interest tests.

Chapter 4
Compliance Programmes

A common theme in the legal regimes associated with the FCPA and UK Bribery Act is the need for an entity to develop, implement and actively enforce an effective compliance programme. Under the UK Bribery Act, an effective compliance programme can serve as a complete defence for an entity subject to its terms. Though the FCPA does not explicitly provide for a similar defence, in practice the existence and effectiveness of a compliance programme are critical factors in making enforcement decisions. For entities subject to the FCPA's accounting and record-keeping provisions, an effective compliance programme is also required as part of an entity's legal obligation to implement adequate internal controls.

With the implementation and increasing enforcement of domestic legislation associated with a series of international anti-bribery conventions, the scope of individuals and entities subject to legal regimes similar to the FCPA and UK Bribery Act is constantly expanding. Aside from the legal mandates, prudence and good business practice dictate that entities engaged in international business put in place effective compliance programmes. Otherwise, an entity's ability to engage in international business can be seriously compromised.

A. Harmonising FCPA and UK Bribery Act Compliance Programmes

Given the breadth of their scope and the extent of their extraterritorial reach, few individuals and entities engaged in international business are beyond the reach of the FCPA and UK Bribery Act. For individuals and entities not directly subject to their terms, they may, in various ways, become otherwise subject to the FCPA and UK Bribery Act as an accomplice. As opposed to focusing on complying with one of the legal regimes, the better practice for entities engaged in international business is to harmonise their compliance programmes to ensure compliance with both the FCPA and UK Bribery Act.

1. Reconciling the Key Differences

In terms of identifying the difference between the FCPA's anti-bribery provisions and the UK Bribery Act, their differences are relatively narrow. The differences are further narrowed when the implications of ancillary legislation are taken into consideration.

a. Facilitating Payments

The UK Bribery Act does not provide an express exception for facilitating payments like the FCPA. While there is uncertainty as to the degree to which facilitating payments will be prosecuted in the UK, the better course for any entity is to prohibit facilitation payments. This also represents the direction of international developments and much of the domestic legislation being implemented and enforced in many countries.

b. Private Bribery

The UK Bribery Act extends its prohibitions to private bribery as well as to the bribery of FPOs. Though the FCPA's prohibitions do not extend to private bribery, other US statutes, such as the Travel Act and, indirectly, the mail and wire fraud statutes, may also apply to private bribery in foreign settings. An entity's compliance programme should extend to prohibiting private bribery as well as the bribery of FPOs. This also has the advantage of avoiding the uncertainty as well as the time and expense associated with determining whether payments are made to officials of state-owned or state-controlled entities.

c. Political Parties, Party Officials, or Candidates for Public Office

The UK Bribery Act does not specifically apply to improper inducements to political parties, party officials or candidates for public office. But its provisions relating to private bribery may be applicable. The FCPA's anti-bribery provisions specifically apply to each of these categories of individuals. A compliance programme should therefore extend its prohibitions to this broader category of individuals.

d. Scope of International Organisations

Because the definition of an international organisation is broader under the UK Bribery Act than under the FCPA, the broader and more inclusive definition should be used. The definition should be broad enough to encompass any international organisation that may possibly be subject to the provisions of either statute.

2. Incorporating Related Considerations

Neither the UK Bribery Act nor the FCPA's anti-bribery provisions directly address accounting and record-keeping issues associated with deterring the risk of bribery and corruption. Nevertheless, the FCPA's accounting and record-keeping provisions and the legal regimes in the UK associated with accounting and record-keeping may have a bearing on an entity's exposure to bribery and corruption risks.

a. Record-Keeping

The record-keeping requirements of the FCPA are limited to a category of entities subject to the jurisdiction of the SEC. Yet their provisions extend to foreign and domestic subsidiaries of entities subject to their terms where the parent has a majority interest or effective control. When consideration is given to the degree to which individuals and entities can be and have been subject to enforcement activity arising out of their status as accomplices, the reach of the FCPA's record-keeping provisions is far broader than is suggested by their terms.

The UK Bribery Act does not contain similar provisions. However, the Companies Acts have been used as a basis to proceed against companies in the UK for activities outside of the UK involving allegations of foreign bribery. As a result, accurate record-keeping is considered to be essential to deterring the likelihood of improper inducements.

b. Internal Controls

Implementing adequate internal controls is a broad concept that establishes an affirmative duty on the part of entities subject to the FCPA's accounting and record-keeping provisions or to the jurisdiction of the UK's Financial Conduct Authority ('FCA'). In each jurisdiction, concepts associated with internal controls are similar and, indeed, overlap with those relating to compliance programmes. For this reason, regardless of whether an entity is subject to the internal control provisions of the FCPA or the FCA's jurisdiction, concepts associated with internal controls should be incorporated into a compliance programme.

B. Critical Components of a Compliance Programme

The basic contours of an effective internal compliance program should resemble those set forth in the US Federal Sentencing Guidelines for organisations, the recently issued FCPA Resource Guide issued by the Justice Department and SEC and the UK Government's Guidance.

In developing an effective compliance programme, it may be helpful to review many of the considerations raised in the guidelines issued by the FCA as well as the decisions and the settlements reached by enforcement authorities in the US and the UK. In this regard, the guidance being issued in various forms by other countries and respected international organisations may also be helpful.

A critical factor in evaluating any compliance programme is whether the programme is adequately designed for maximum effectiveness in preventing and detecting wrongdoing by employees and others acting on an entity's behalf. Another critical factor is whether management is sincerely and actively enforcing the compliance programme or, alternatively, tacitly or selectively disregarding the compliance programme in pressuring employees and others to achieve business objectives.

A compliance programme must be more than a 'paper program' and much more than a series of policies and procedures. Employees must be adequately informed about the compliance programme and be convinced of an entity's commitment to it. A compliance programme must be designed, implemented, reviewed and revised, as appropriate, to ensure its effectiveness.

1. Commitment from the Top

An entity's top management, by example and deed, must be committed to instituting a culture of compliance to deter prohibited conduct by individuals and entities associated with it. No different than business and financial risks, corruption-related risks should be among the range of factors considered by senior management in making business decisions.

- ❑ *Senior management should adopt a public policy of zero tolerance of bribery.*
- ❑ *Senior management should treat bribery and corruption risks in the same manner as other risks faced by an entity.*
  Compliance officials should have a role in the process of evaluating business opportunities.
- ❑ *Senior management should be actively engaged in an entity's approach to addressing bribery and corruption risks.*
  - ❑ Strategies and policies for managing and monitoring the risk of bribery or corruption should be approved and periodically reviewed at a senior level.
  - ❑ Prompt and effective responses should be taken to significant bribery and corruption events to improve systems and controls and various aspects of compliance programmes.
- ❑ *Senior management should ensure that policies and procedures are applied consistently and effectively.*
  - ❑ Senior management should ensure that policies and procedures are clear and appropriate and communicated throughout an entity's organisation.
  - ❑ Disciplinary measures should be applied consistently against senior and lower-level officials as well as employees, agents and other intermediaries.
- ❑ *Senior management should promote accountability and assign clear responsibility.*

❑   One or more specific senior and respected members of management should be designated and assigned responsibility for overseeing and implementing a compliance programme. Individuals assigned compliance responsibilities should have appropriate experience as well as clear reporting lines.

❑   Senior management should be engaged with the oversight process and ensure that decisions on the allocation of compliance, audit and other resources are adequate and risk-based.

❑   *Senior management should promote coordination and information sharing across the organisation.*

❑   Senior management and oversight officials should be provided critical information on a timely basis.

❑   Compliance officials should have full access to the due diligence conducted on business opportunities.

2. Policies and Proportionate Procedures

An entity should put in place up-to-date policies and procedures appropriate to the circumstances associated with the business it conducts. Policies and procedures should not be simply adopted from another entity, or from model forms, or simply consist of codes of conduct.

❑   *Policies and procedures should be tailored to address the particular needs of an entity.*

❑   Policies and procedures should be proportionate to the risks of corruption an entity faces and be designed to address the nature, scale and complexity of an entity's activities.

❑   Policies and procedures should be communicated to individuals and entities and be readily accessible to all employees and those conducting business on an entity's behalf.

❑   *Policies and procedures should be clear, concise and understandable to all employees and to those conducting business on an entity's behalf.*

❑   Policies and procedures should be sufficiently clear and understandable to a person unsophisticated or unfamiliar with the relevant issues and conveyed in the local language with practical examples to help explain the policies and procedures.

❑ Policies and procedures should address relevant areas of concern without becoming unduly burdensome, unresponsive or unable to adjust to ever-changing needs.

❑ *Policies and procedures should outline responsibilities within an entity and set out disciplinary procedures.*

   ❑ The policies and procedures should extend to any individual or entity acting on an entity's behalf.

   ❑ The policies and procedures should be designed to help an entity identify whether someone acting on its behalf is corrupt.

3. Record-Keeping

As a matter of policy and practice, accurate record-keeping should be required throughout an entity's organisation. An entity's ability to implement and monitor its compliance programme is highly dependent upon the accuracy of its records and the effectiveness of its record-keeping practices.

❑ *Records should in reasonable detail accurately and fairly reflect the true nature of a transaction.*

   Reliance upon generic descriptions and explanations should not be permitted.

❑ *Adequate procedures should be put in place to ensure that there is adequate specificity in the records of the third party as to the reasons for or purposes of third-party payments.*

   Adequate documentation and other material information should be required before making payments.

4. Risk Assessment

An entity should identify, assess and regularly review and update its exposure to potential external and internal bribery and corruption risks on its behalf and adjust its procedures and concentrate its resources accordingly.

❑ *Risk-based, appropriate additional monitoring and due diligence should take place for jurisdictions, sectors and business relationships identified as higher risk.*

   ❑ Consideration should be given to risks associated with the products and services being offered, the jurisdictions where business is conducted and the business practices in those jurisdictions.

   ❑ An entity's approach to providing corporate hospitality, to making charitable and political donations and to relying on the use of third parties should be regularly assessed.

❑ *The risk of staff or third parties acting on the entity's behalf should be addressed across the business, including all jurisdictions where the entity operates through third parties and across all business channels.*

   ❑ Among the factors that should be kept in mind is whether staff in higher risk positions are becoming vulnerable to violating policies and procedures.

   ❑ Risks are to be addressed in a coordinated manner across the business and information should be readily shared.

❑ *Incentive or remuneration structures should be addressed to ensure that they do not increase the risk of bribery and corruption.*

   ❑ An entity should not have bonus structures for staff in higher risk positions that are linked to the amount of income or profit they produce, particularly when bonuses form a major part of their remuneration.

   ❑ Compliance issues should be tied to promotions, bonuses and other incentives and not solely tied to income-related or profit-related considerations.

❑ *An entity should on a regular and on-going basis assess the nature and extent of its exposure to potential external and internal risks of corruption of individuals and entities associated with it.*

   ❑ Regular assessments of bribery and corruption risks should be taken with a specific senior person responsible for ensuring these assessments are done, taking into account the country and class of business involved as well as other relevant factors.

❑   Steps should be taken to ensure that review teams undertaking the assessments have sufficient knowledge of relevant issues and, where necessary, external expertise should be sought.

❑   *Staff should be vetted on a risk-based approach taking into account the seriousness and relevance of the risk in the context of the individual's role or proposed role.*

❑   Enhanced vetting should not only take place for senior staff when more junior staff are working in positions where they could be exposed to bribery or corruption risks.

❑   Temporary or contract staff should not receive less vigorous vetting than permanent staff carrying out similar roles.

❑   *Risks should be assessed and addressed in a good faith manner.*

❑   A dispassionate consideration of all relevant factors should be required. Simply checking the boxes in a perfunctory manner in filling out a series of forms is inadequate.

❑   An entity should not rely exclusively on informal means or general perceptions to assess bribery and corruption risks.

5. The Compliance Function

Responsibility for anti-bribery and corruption systems and controls should be clear and documented and assigned to a single senior manager or to a committee with senior management membership, with appropriate terms of reference, who or which reports ultimately to the board or to a similar oversight body.

❑   *Due diligence should be adjusted in a proportionate manner to address the level of risk and the circumstances unique to each situation.*

Resources should be allocated to address situations where the risks are the greatest. A 'one-size-fits-all' approach to due diligence should be avoided.

❑   *Compliance officials assigned responsibility should have appropriate seniority and experience as well as clear reporting lines.*

❑   The compliance official or officials assigned primary responsibility should be well-respected and have significant seniority within an entity's organisation.

❑   Compliance and internal audit staff should have sufficient competence in terms of experience and specialised training to address relevant compliance issues.

❑   *Compliance officials should have adequate autonomy from management and sufficient resources to ensure that an entity's compliance programme is implemented effectively.*

    ❑   Compliance officials should have direct access to an entity's governing authority, such as the board of directors and committees of the board of directors.

    ❑   Adequate staffing and resources need to be provided and, whenever necessary, an entity should bolster insufficient knowledge or resources with external expertise.

❑   *An entity's compliance function should have oversight of all third-party relationships.*

Third-party relationships should be reviewed and approved by compliance officials in addition to being monitored by compliance officials on an on-going basis.

6. Implementing Policies and Procedures

Policies and procedures should be communicated and actively enforced throughout an entity, including with respect to agents, partners or collaborating entities.

❑   *Disciplinary procedures should be clear and applied consistently and promptly.*

No one should be exempted from policies or procedures or from disciplinary action.

❑   *Adequate resources should be provided so that allegations can be properly and quickly investigated and appropriate measures taken.*

Sufficient staff should be in place to audit, document, analyse and utilize the results of an entity's compliance efforts as well as to conduct internal investigations.

7. Training

Training needs should be appropriately tailored to meet an entity's needs as well as the needs of the targeted audience. Entities should review employees' competence and take appropriate action to ensure that they remain competent for their roles.

❑ *An entity should regularly review and identify training needs to ensure that the training is adequate and proportionate to the risks.*

   ❑ Training should not be neglected in the belief that various controls are sufficient to combat bribery and corruption risks.

   ❑ Higher-risk roles should be subject to more thorough vetting and training.

❑ *An entity should satisfy itself that its staff understands their responsibilities.*

   ❑ An entity should regularly test the understanding of staff and use the results to assess individual training needs and the overall quality of the training.

   ❑ An entity should evaluate an employee's likely exposure to risks in conjunction with his or her responsibilities and whether the employee is competent and otherwise capable of carrying out preventive functions effectively.

❑ *Training, including refresher training and training materials, should be of consistent quality, up-to-date and appropriate to an employee's role.*

   ❑ Training should be practical and include examples of risks and how to comply with policies and procedures. It should not dwell unduly on legislation and regulations.

   ❑ Staff responsible for training should have adequate training themselves.

❑ *Whistleblowing and procedures to escalate concerns to higher levels should be part of training and should clearly communicate how to report suspicions or how to raise concerns with staff.*

Alternative reporting routes should be provided for staff wishing to make a whistleblowing disclosure about their line management or senior managers.

8. Seeking Guidance and Advice

Measures should be implemented to ensure that timely advice can be sought and provided to facilitate compliance with an entity's policies and procedures.

❏ *An entity should encourage employees to seek guidance from more senior officials with the requisite expertise when confronted with unclear or complex situations.*

    ❏ Staff without the requisite expertise should not be placed in situations to make a determination relative to compliance issues without having ready access to staff with the necessary expertise.

    ❏ Challenging situations should be promptly elevated to higher levels within an entity to staff with the requisite expertise.

❏ *Procedures should be put in place so that knowledgeable officials can quickly answer questions and respond to concerns.*

    ❏ To enhance the likelihood that guidance will be sought and corrective action taken, procedures should not be cumbersome or perceived as being punitive in nature.

    ❏ Genuine efforts should be made to ensure that anyone seeking to secure guidance or to make appropriate disclosures is not subject to retaliation.

❏ *An entity should have whistleblowing procedures that are clear and accessible and that respect staff confidentiality.*

    ❏ A compliance programme should include a mechanism for reporting suspected misconduct on a confidential basis.

    ❏ Policies should be implemented to ensure that no one making a confidential disclosure fears retaliation.

9. Monitoring

On an on-going basis, a compliance program should be monitored, regularly reviewed and modified as necessary to address weaknesses and to be made more effective.

❏ *A compliance programme should be regularly tested and reviewed to identify weaknesses, to adjust to changing circumstances and risks and to develop ways of improving its efficiency and effectiveness.*

❑ Policies and procedures should be regularly reviewed and updated on a timely basis to address emerging risks and recent events.

❑ Audit findings and compliance lessons should be shared between and among business units.

❑ *Care should be exercised to ensure that policies and procedures are applied consistently and effectively.*

❑ The effectiveness of policies, procedures, systems and controls should be monitored by senior management, compliance officials and internal audit staff.

❑ Effective compliance monitoring and internal audit reviews should challenge not only whether processes to mitigate bribery and corruption have been followed but also the effectiveness of the processes themselves.

10. Third Parties

Entities should take risk-sensitive measures to address the risk that a third party acting on behalf of the entity may engage in questionable practices. Criteria and mechanisms should be developed to determine the degree of due diligence required.

❑ *An entity should know its third parties and policies and procedures should be established relative to their selection on a risk-sensitive basis.*

❑ Higher or extra levels of due diligence and approvals should be required for higher-risk, third-party relationships, especially when third parties are used to introduce or generate business.

❑ Reasonable steps should be taken to verify the information provided by third parties during the due diligence process.

❑ The qualifications and associations of third parties must be understood and documented as well as the business rationale for using the third party. Vague explanations should not be accepted.

❑ Those approving third-party relationships should not have a conflict of interest or be perceived as not being in a position to make a dispassionate decision.

❑ *Compliance obligations should be disclosed and commitments obtained from third parties.*

    ❑ When third parties are being considered as intermediaries, an entity should satisfy itself that a third party has an adequate compliance programme to detect and prevent bribery.

    ❑ Compliance provisions should be required in agreements governing relationships with third parties, especially in higher risk situations.

❑ *Due diligence on third parties should be documented.* Accurate and updated central records should be maintained of approved third parties, the due diligence conducted on the relationship and the evidence of periodic reviews.

    ❑ The due diligence process should be applied consistently when establishing and reviewing third-party relationships.

    ❑ Affirmative measures taken to minimize bribery and corruption risks, such as compliance provisions in written agreements, specialised controls and other affirmative steps, should be documented and considered as part of the due diligence process.

❑ *Third-party relationships should be monitored on an on-going basis, especially in high-risk areas.*

    ❑ Follow-up steps should be taken to ensure that the business reasons for using the third party are supported by the terms of any agreements, by the timing and manner in which payments are made and by there being verification of the work performed.

    ❑ An entity should review in sufficient detail its relationships with third parties on a regular basis to confirm that it is still necessary and appropriate to continue with the relationship. Long-standing third-party relationships should not be presumed to present no bribery or corruption risks.

❑ *Regular and thorough monitoring of third-party payments should take place.*

    ❑ Guidelines should be set that take into account the risk factors associated with the role of a third party. Procedures should be instituted to impose limits, and criteria for approval, on different types of expenditures, such as gifts, hospitality and commissions.

❑   Adequate due diligence and approval of third-party relationships should take place before payments are made to a third party.

❑   An entity should be able to produce a list of approved third parties, associated due diligence and details of payments made to them.

❑   Third parties should be paid directly for their work and not in cash.

❑   Payments to third parties should be adequately documented so that there is a clear audit trail.

❑ *Third Party Bank Accounts*

    ❑   Reasonable steps should be taken to ensure that bank accounts used by third parties to receive payments are actually controlled by the third party for whom the payment is meant.

    ❑   Instructions from third parties should not be accepted to make a payment to other individuals or entities which have not been subject to due diligence.

11. Mergers and Acquisitions

Thorough due diligence for corruption risks should be performed as part of mergers and acquisitions.

❑ *Pre-Acquisition Due Diligence*

  It should not be assumed that third-party relationships acquired from other entities have been subject to adequate due diligence.

❑ *Post-Acquisition Integration*

  The acquired entity should be fully integrated into the internal controls and compliance programme of the acquiring entity. This would extend to all aspects of compliance, such as evaluating and monitoring third parties, training employees and expanding audits to the newly merged or acquired entity.

Appendix A

Excerpt - A Resource Guide To The U.S. Foreign Corrupt Practices Act ('FCPA Resource Guide')*

* * *

Corporate Compliance Program

In a global marketplace, an effective compliance program is a critical component of a company's internal controls and is essential to detecting and preventing FCPA violations.[300] Effective compliance programs are tailored to the company's specific business and to the risks associated with that business. They are dynamic and evolve as the business and the markets change.

An effective compliance program promotes "an organizational culture that encourages ethical conduct and a commitment to compliance with the law."[301] Such a program protects a company's reputation, ensures investor value and confidence, reduces uncertainty in business transactions, and

---

* U.S. Dep't Of Justice And Sec. & Exch. Comm'n, *A Resource Guide to the U.S. Foreign Corrupt Practices Act* (Nov. 2012), *available at* http://www.justice.gov/criminal/fraud/fcpa/guide.pdf.

300. *See* U.S. Sentencing Guidelines at § 8B2.1(a)(2).
301. U.S. Sentencing Guidelines § 8B2.1(b).

secures a company's assets.[302] A well-constructed, thoughtfully implemented, and consistently enforced compliance and ethics program helps prevent, detect, remediate, and report misconduct, including FCPA violations.

In addition to considering whether a company has self-reported, cooperated, and taken appropriate remedial actions, DOJ and SEC also consider the adequacy of a company's compliance program when deciding what, if any, action to take. The program may influence whether or not charges should be resolved through a deferred prosecution agreement (DPA) or non-prosecution agreement (NPA), as well as the appropriate length of any DPA or NPA, or the term of corporate probation. It will often affect the penalty amount and the need for a monitor or self-reporting.[303] As discussed above, SEC's *Seaboard Report* focuses, among other things, on a company's self-policing prior to the discovery of the misconduct, including whether it had established effective compliance procedures.[304] Likewise,

---

302. *See generally* DEBBIE TROKLUS, ET AL, COMPLIANCE 101: HOW TO BUILD AND MAINTAIN AN EFFECTIVE COMPLIANCE AND ETHICS PROGRAM, SOCIETY OF CORP. COMPLIANCE AND ETHICS (2008) 3-9 [hereinafter COMPLIANCE 101] (listing reasons to implement compliance program, including protecting company's reputation, creating trust between management and employees, preventing false statements to customers, creating efficiencies and streamlining processes, detecting employee and contractor fraud and abuse, ensuring high-quality products and services, and providing "early warning" system of inappropriate actions); TRANSPARENCY INT'L, BUSINESS PRINCIPLES FOR COUNTERING BRIBERY: SMALL AND MEDIUM ENTERPRISE (SME) (EDITION 5 (2008) (citing benefits of anti-bribery program like protecting reputation, creating record of integrity enhances opportunities to acquire government business, protecting company assets otherwise squandered on bribes); MARK PIETH, HARMONISING ANTI-CORRUPTION COMPLIANCE: THE OECD GOOD PRACTICE GUIDANCE 45-46 (2011) [hereinafter HARMONISING ANTI-CORRUPTION COMPLIANCE] (citing need for compliance program to prevent and detect in-house risks, such as workplace security or conflicts of interest, and external risks, like anti-trust violations, embargo circumvention, environmental hazards, and money laundering).

303. Debarment authorities, such as the Department of Defense or the General Services Administration, may also consider a company's compliance program when deciding whether to debar or suspend a contractor. Specifically, the relevant regulations provide that the debarment authority should consider "[w]hether the contractor had effective standards of conduct and internal control systems in place at the time of the activity which constitutes cause for debarment or had adopted such procedures prior to any Government investigation of the activity cited as a cause for debarment," and "[w]hether the contractor has instituted or agreed to institute new or revised review and control procedures and ethics training programs." 48 C.F.R. § 9.406-1(a).

304. [U.S. SEC. AND EXCHANGE COMM., REPORT OF INVESTIGATION PURSUANT TO SECTION 21(A) OF THE SECURITIES EXCHANGE ACT OF 1934 AND COMMISSION STATEMENT ON THE RELATIONSHIP ON THE RELATIONSHIP OF COOPERATION TO AGENCY ENFORCEMENT DECISIONS, SEC Rel. Nos. 34-44969 and AAER-1470 (Oct. 23, 2001), *available at* http://www.

three of the nine factors set forth in DOJ's *Principles of Federal Prosecution of Business Organizations* relate, either directly or indirectly, to a compliance program's design and implementation, including the pervasiveness of wrongdoing within the company, the existence and effectiveness of the company's pre-existing compliance program, and the company's remedial actions.[305] DOJ also considers the U.S. Sentencing Guidelines' elements of an effective compliance program, as set forth in § 8B2.1 of the Guidelines.

These considerations reflect the recognition that a company's failure to prevent every single violation does not necessarily mean that a particular company's compliance program was not generally effective. DOJ and SEC understand that "no compliance program can ever prevent all criminal activity by a corporation's employees,"[306] and they do not hold companies to a standard of perfection. An assessment of a company's compliance program, including its design and good faith implementation and enforcement, is an important part of the government's assessment of whether a violation occurred, and if so, what action should be taken. In appropriate circumstances, DOJ and SEC may decline to pursue charges against a company based on the company's effective compliance program, or may otherwise

---

sec.gov/litigation/investreport/34-44969.htm]; U.S. Sec. and Exchange Comm., Report of Investigation Pursuant to Section 21(A) of the Securities Exchange Act of 1934 and Commission Statement on the Relationship of Cooperation to Agency Enforcement Decisions, SEC Rel. No. 44969 (Oct. 23, 2001), *available at* http://www.sec.gov/litigation/investreport/34-44969.htm.

305. USAM § 9-28.300. When evaluating the pervasiveness of wrongdoing within the corporation, prosecutors are advised that while it may be appropriate to charge a corporation for minor misconduct where the wrongdoing was pervasive, "it may not be appropriate to impose liability upon a corporation, *particularly one with a robust compliance program in place,* under a strict *respondent superior* theory for the single isolated act of a rogue employee." *Id.*§ 9-28.500.A (emphasis added). Prosecutors should also consider a company's compliance program when examining any remedial actions taken, including efforts to implement an effective compliance program or to improve an existing one. As the commentary explains, "although the inadequacy of a corporate compliance program is a factor to consider when deciding whether to charge a corporation, that corporation's quick recognition of the flaws in the program and its efforts to improve the program are also factors to consider as to appropriate disposition of a case." *Id.*§ 9-28.900.B. Finally, the Principles of Federal Prosecution of Business Organizations provides that prosecutors should consider the existence and effectiveness of the corporation's pre-existing compliance program in determining how to treat a corporate target. *Id.* § 9-28.800.

306. *See* USAM § 9-28.800.B; *see also* U.S. Sentencing Guidelines § 8B2.1(a) (2011) ("The failure to prevent or detect the instant offense does not necessarily mean that the program is not generally effective in preventing and detecting criminal conduct.").

seek to reward a company for its program, even when that program did not prevent the particular underlying FCPA violation that gave rise to the investigation.[307]

DOJ and SEC have no formulaic requirements regarding compliance programs. Rather, they employ a common-sense and pragmatic approach to evaluating compliance programs, making inquiries related to three basic questions:

- Is the company's compliance program well designed?
- Is it being applied in good faith?
- Does it work?[308]

This guide contains information regarding some of the basic elements DOJ and SEC consider when evaluating compliance programs. Although the focus is on compliance with the FCPA, given the existence of anti-corruption laws in many other countries, businesses should consider designing programs focused on anti-corruption compliance more broadly.[309]

---

307. *See* Press Release, U.S. Dept. of Justice, Former Morgan Stanley Managing Director Pleads Guilty for Role in Evading Internal Controls Required by FCPA (Apr. 25, 2012) (declining to bring criminal case against corporate employer that "had constructed and maintained a system of internal controls, which provided reasonable assurances that its employees were not bribing government officials"), *available at* http://www.justice.gov/opa/pr/2012/April/12-crm-534.html; Press Release, U.S. Sec. and Exchange Comm., SEC Charges Former Morgan Stanley Executive with FCPA Violations and Investment Advisor Fraud, No. 2012-78 (Apr. 25, 2012) (indicating corporate employer was not charged in the matter and had "cooperated with the SEC's inquiry and conducted a thorough internal investigation to determine the scope of the improper payments and other misconduct involved"), *available at* http://www.sec.gov/newspress/2012/2012-78.htm.

308. *See* USAM § 9-28.800.B.

309. *See, e.g.,* INT'L CHAMBER OF COMMERCE, ICC RULES ON COMBATING CORRUPTION (2011) [hereinafter ICC RULES ON COMBATTING CORRUPTION], *available at* http://www.iccwbo.org/uploadedFiles/ICC/policy/business_in_society/Statements/ICC_Rules_on_Combating_Corruption_2011edition.pdf; TRANSPARENCY INT'L, BUSINESS PRINCIPLES FOR COUNTERING BRIBERY (2d ed. 2009) [hereinafter BUSINESS PRINCIPLES FOR COUNTERING BRIBERY], *available at* http://www.transparency.org/global_priorities/private_sector/business_principles/; UNITED KINGDOM MINISTRY OF JUSTICE, THE BRIBERY ACT OF 2010, GUIDANCE ABOUT PROCEDURES WHICH RELEVANT COMMERCIAL ORGANISATIONS CAN PUT IN PLACE TO PREVENT PERSONS ASSOCIATED WITH THEM FROM BRIBERY (2010), *available at* http://www.justice.gov.uk/downloads/legislation/bribery-act-2010-guidance.pdf; WORLD BANK GROUP, INTEGRITY COMPLIANCE GUIDELINES (2011) [hereinafter INTEGRITY COMPLIANCE GUIDELINES], *available at* http://sitereousrces.worldbank.org/INTDOII/Resources/Integrity_Compliance_Guidelines.

Hallmarks of Effective Compliance Programs

Individual companies may have different compliance needs depending on their size and the particular risks associated with their businesses, among other factors. When it comes to compliance, there is no one-size-fits-all program. Thus, the discussion below is meant to provide insight into the aspects of compliance programs that DOJ and SEC assess, recognizing that companies may consider a variety of factors when making their own determination of what is appropriate for their specific business needs.[310] Indeed, small-and-medium-size enterprises likely will have different compliance programs from large multi-national corporations, a fact DOJ and SEC take into account when evaluating companies' compliance programs.

Compliance programs that employ a "check-the-box" approach may be inefficient and, more importantly, ineffective. Because each compliance program should be tailored to an organization's specific needs, risks, and challenges, the information provided below should not be considered a substitute for a company's own assessment of the corporate compliance program most appropriate for that particular business organization. In the end, if designed carefully, implemented earnestly, and enforced fairly, a company's compliance program—no matter how large or small the organization—will

---

pdf; Asia-Pacific Economic Cooperation, APEC Anti-Corruption Code of Conduct for Business (2007) [hereinafter APEC Anti-Corruption Code], *available at* www.apec.org/ Groups/SOM-Steering-Committee-on-Economic-and-Technical-Cooperation/Task-Groups/~/ media/Files/Groups/ACT/07_act_codebrochure.ashx; Int'l Chamber of Commerce, Transparency Int'l, United Nation Global Compact, and World Economic Forum, Resisting Extortion and Solicitation in International Transactions: A Company Tool for Employee Training (2011), *available at* http://www3.weforum.org/docs/WEF_PACI_RESIST_ Report_2011.pdf; World Economic Forum, Partnering Against Corruption – Principles for Countering Bribery (2009) [hereinafter Partnering Against Corruption], *available at* http://www3.weforum.org/docs/WEF_PACI_Principles_2009.pdf; Working Group on Bribery, OECD, Good Practice Guidance on Internal Controls, Ethics, and Compliance 2010, [hereinafter OECD Good Practice Guidance] *available at* http://www.oecd. org/dataoecd/5/51/44884389.pdf; U.N. Global Compact, The Ten Principles [hereinafter The Ten Principles], *available at* http://www.unglobalcompact.org/aboutTheGC/TheTen-Principles/index.html.

310. This is also reflected in the *Sentencing Guidelines*, which recognizes that no single, formulaic set of requirements should be imposed, but instead focuses on a number of factors like applicable industry practice or the standards called for by any applicable governmental regulations, the size of the organization, and whether the organization has engaged in similar misconduct in the past. *See* U.S. Sentencing Guidelines § 8b2.1 & app. note 2 (2011).

allow the company generally to prevent violations, detect those that do occur, and remediate them promptly and appropriately.

Commitment from Senior Management and a Clearly Articulated Policy Against Corruption

Within a business organization, compliance begins with the board of directors and senior executives setting the proper tone for the rest of the company. Managers and employees take their cues from these corporate leaders. Thus, DOJ and SEC consider the commitment of corporate leaders to a "culture of compliance"[311] and look to see if this high-level commitment is also reinforced and implemented by middle managers and employees at all levels of a business. A well-designed compliance program that is not enforced in good faith, such as when corporate management explicitly or implicitly encourages employees to engage in misconduct to achieve business objectives, will be ineffective. DOJ and SEC have often encountered companies with compliance programs that are strong on paper but that nevertheless have significant FCPA violations because management has failed to effectively implement the program even in the face of obvious signs of corruption. This may be the result of aggressive sales staff preventing compliance personnel from doing their jobs effectively and of senior management, more concerned with securing a valuable business opportunity than enforcing a culture of compliance, siding with the sales team. The higher the financial stakes of the transaction, the greater the temptation for management to choose profit over compliance.

A strong ethical culture directly supports a strong compliance program. By adhering to ethical standards, senior managers will inspire middle managers to reinforce those standards. Compliant middle managers, in turn,

---

311. This was understood by then-SEC Commissioner Cynthia Glassman in 2003 in a speech on the SEC's implementation of the Sarbanes-Oxley Act: "[T]he ultimate effectiveness of the new corporate governance rules will be determined by the 'tone at the top'. Adopting a code of ethics means little if the company's chief executive officer or its directors make clear, by conduct or otherwise, that the code's provisions do not apply to them . . . Corporate officers and directors hold the ultimate power and responsibility for restoring public trust by conducting themselves in a manner that is worthy of the trust that is placed in them." Cynthia Glassman, SEC Implementation of Sarbanes-Oxley: The New Corporate Governance, Remarks at National Economists Club (April 7, 2003), *available at* http://www.sec.gov/news/speech/spch040703cag.htm.

will encourage employees to strive to attain those standards throughout the organizational structure.[312]

In short, compliance with the FCPA and ethical rules must start at the top. DOJ and SEC thus evaluate whether senior management has clearly articulated company standards, communicated them in unambiguous terms, adhered to them scrupulously, and disseminated them throughout the organization.

Code of Conduct and Compliance Policies and Procedures

A company's code of conduct is often the foundation upon which an effective compliance program is built. As DOJ has repeatedly noted in its charging documents, the most effective codes are clear, concise, and accessible to all employees and to those conducting business on the company's behalf. Indeed it would be difficult to effectively implement a compliance program if it was not available in the local language so that employees in foreign subsidiaries can access and understand it. When assessing a compliance program, DOJ and SEC will review whether the company has taken steps to make certain that the code of conduct remains current and effective and whether a company has periodically reviewed and updated its code.

Whether a company has policies and procedures that outline responsibilities for compliance within the company, detail proper internal controls, auditing practices, and documentation policies, and set forth disciplinary procedures will also be considered by DOJ and SEC. These types of policies

---

312. Indeed, research has found that "[e]thical culture is the single biggest factor determining the amount of misconduct that will take place in a business." ETHICS RESOURCE CENTER, 2009 NATIONAL BUSINESS ETHICS SURVEY: ETHICS IN RECESSION (2009), at 41. Metrics of ethical culture include ethical leadership (tone at the top), supervisor reinforcement of ethical behavior (middle management reinforcement), and peer commitment (supporting one another in doing the right thing). ETHICS RESOURCE CENTER 2011, NATIONAL BUSINESS ETHICS SURVEY: WORKPLACE ETHICS IN TRANSITION (2012) at 19. Strong ethical cultures and strong ethics and compliance programs are related, as data show that a well-implemented program helps lead to a strong ethical culture. *Id.* at 34. "Understanding the nature of any gap between the desired culture and the actual culture is a critical first step in determining the nature of any ethics-based risks inside the organization." David Gebler, *The Role of Culture* at 1.7, *in* SOCIETY OF CORPORATE COMPLIANCE AND ETHICS, THE COMPLETE CORPORATE COMPLIANCE AND ETHICS MANUAL (2011). To create an ethical culture, attention must be paid to norms at all levels of an organization, including the "tone at the top," "mood in the middle," and "buzz at the bottom." *Id.* at 1.9-1.10.

and procedures will depend on the size and nature of the business and the risk associated with the business. Effective policies and procedures require an in-depth understanding of the company's business model, including its products and services, third-party agents, customers, government interactions, and industry and geographic risks. Among the risks that a company may need to address include the nature and extent of transactions with foreign governments, including payment to foreign officials; use of third parties; gifts, travel and entertainment expenses; charitable and political donations; and facilitating and expediting payments. For example, some companies with global operations have created web-based approval processes to review and approve routine gifts, travel, and entertainment involving foreign officials and private customers with clear monetary limits and annual limitations. Many of these systems have built-in flexibility so that senior management, or in-house counsel, can be apprised of and, in appropriate circumstances, approve unique requests. These types of systems can be a good way to conserve corporate resources while, if properly implemented, preventing and detecting potential FCPA violations.

Regardless of the specific policies and procedures implemented, these standards should apply to personnel at all levels of the company.

Oversight, Autonomy, and Resources

In appraising a compliance program, DOJ and SEC also consider whether a company has assigned a responsibility for the oversight and implementation of a company's compliance program to one or more specific senior executives within an organization.[313] Those individuals must have appropriate authority within the organization, adequate autonomy from management, and sufficient resources to ensure that the company's compliance program is implemented effectively.[314] Adequate autonomy generally includes direct access to an organization's governing authority, such as the board of directors and committees of the board of directors (e.g., the audit committee).[315] Depending on the size and structure of an organization, it may be appro-

---

313. *See, e.g.,* U.S. Sentencing Guidelines § 8B2.1(2)(B)-(C) (2011).
314. *Id.*
315. *Id.*

priate for day-to-day operational responsibility to be delegated to other specific individuals within a company.[316] DOJ and SEC recognize that the reporting structure will depend on the size and complexity of an organization. Moreover, the amount of resources devoted to compliance will depend on the company's size, complexity, industry, geographical reach, and risks associated with the business. In assessing whether a company has reasonable internal controls, DOJ and SEC typically consider whether the company devoted adequate staffing and resources to the compliance program given the size, structure, and risk profile of the business.

Risk Assessment

Assessment of risk is fundamental to developing a strong compliance program, and is another factor DOJ and SEC evaluate when assessing a company's compliance program.[317] One-size-fits-all compliance programs are generally ill-conceived and ineffective because resources inevitably are spread too thin, with too much focus on low-risk markets and transactions to the detriment of high-risk areas. Devoting a disproportionate amount of time policing modest entertainment and gift-giving instead of focusing on large government bids, questionable payments to third-party consultants, or excessive discounts to resellers and distributors may indicate that a company's compliance program is ineffective. A $50 million contract with a government agency in a high-risk country warrants greater scrutiny than modest and routine gifts and entertainment. Similarly, performing identical due diligence on all third-party agents, irrespective of risk factors, is often counter-productive, diverting attention and resources away from those third parties that pose the most significant risks. DOJ and SEC will give meaningful credit to a company that implements in good faith a comprehensive, risk-based compliance program, even if that program does not prevent an infraction in a low risk area because greater attention and resources had been devoted to a higher risk area. Conversely, a company that fails to prevent an FCPA violation on an economically significant, high-risk transaction

---

316. *Id.*

317. *See, e.g.,* Ethics and Compliance Officer Association Foundation, the Ethics and Compliance Handbook: A Practical Guide from Leading Organizations (2008) at 13-26 [hereinafter The Ethics and Compliance Handbook].

because it failed to perform a level of due diligence commensurate with the size and risk of the transaction is likely to receive reduced credit based on the quality and effectiveness of its compliance program.

As a company's risk for FCPA violations increases, that business should consider increasing its compliance procedures, including due diligence and periodic internal audits. The degree of appropriate due diligence is fact-specific and should vary based on industry, country, size, and nature of the transaction, and the method and amount of third-party compensation. Factors to consider, for instance, include risks presented by: the country and industry sector, the business opportunity, potential business partners, level of involvement with governments, amount of government regulation and oversight, and exposure to customs and immigration in conducting business affairs. When assessing a company's compliance program, DOJ and SEC take into account whether and to what degree a company analyzes and addresses the particular risks it faces.

Training and Continuing Advice

Compliance policies cannot work unless effectively communicated throughout a company. Accordingly, DOJ and SEC will evaluate whether a company has taken steps to ensure that relevant policies and procedures have been communicated throughout the organization, including through periodic training and certification for all directors, officers, relevant employees, and, where appropriate, agents and business partners.[318] For example, many larger companies have implemented a mix of web-based and in-person training conducted at varying intervals. Such training typically covers company policies and procedures, instruction on applicable laws, practical advice to address real-life scenarios, and case studies. Regardless of how a company chooses to conduct its training, however, the information should be presented in a manner appropriate for the targeted audience, including providing training and training materials in the local language. For example, companies may want to consider providing different types of training to their sales personnel and accounting personnel with hypotheticals or sample situations that are similar to the situations they might encounter.

---

318. *See* U.S. Sentencing Guidelines § 8B2.1(b)(4) (2011).

In addition to the existence and scope of a company's training program, a company should develop appropriate measures, depending on the size and sophistication of the particular company, to provide guidance and advice on complying with the company's ethics and compliance program, including when such advice is needed urgently. Such measures will help ensure that the compliance program is understood and followed appropriately at all levels of the company.

Incentives and Disciplinary Measures

In addition to evaluating the design and implementation of a compliance program throughout an organization, enforcement of that program is fundamental to its effectiveness.[319] A compliance program should apply from the board room to the supply room—no one should be beyond its reach. DOJ and SEC will thus consider whether, when enforcing a compliance program, a company has appropriate and clear disciplinary procedures, whether those procedures are applied reliably and promptly, and whether they are commensurate with the violation. Many companies have found that publicizing disciplinary actions internally, where appropriate under local law, can have an important deterrent effect, demonstrating that unethical and unlawful actions have swift and sure consequences.

DOJ and SEC recognize that positive incentives can also drive compliant behavior. These incentives can take many forms such as personnel evaluations and promotions, rewards for improving and developing a company's compliance program, and rewards for ethics and compliance leadership.[320] Some organizations, for example, have made adherence to compliance a significant metric for management's bonuses so that compliance becomes an integral part of management's everyday concern. Beyond financial incentives, some companies have highlighted compliance within their organizations

---

319. *See* U.S. SENTENCING GUIDELINES § 8B2.1(b)(6) (2011) ("The organization's compliance and ethics program shall be promoted and enforced consistently throughout the organization through (A) appropriate incentives to perform in accordance with the compliance and ethics program; and (B) appropriate disciplinary measures for engaging in criminal conduct and for failing to take reasonable steps to prevent or detect criminal conduct").

320. *See, e.g.*, JOSEPH E. MURPHY, SOCIETY OF CORP. COMPLIANCE AND ETHICS, USING INCENTIVES IN YOUR COMPLIANCE AND ETHICS PROGRAM (2011) at 1; THE ETHICS AND COMPLIANCE HANDBOOK, *supra* note 317, at 111-23.

by recognizing compliance professionals and internal audit staff. Others have made working in the company's compliance organization a way to advance an employee's career. SEC, for instance, has encouraged companies to embrace methods to incentivize ethical and lawful behavior:

> [M]ake integrity, ethics and compliance part of the promotion, compensation and evaluation processes as well. For at the end of the day, the most effective way to communicate that "doing the right thing" is a priority, is to reward it. Conversely, if employees are led to believe that, when it comes to compensation and career advancement, all that counts is short-term profitability, and that cutting ethical corners is an acceptable way of getting there, they'll perform to that measure. To cite an example from a different walk of life: a college football coach can be told that the graduation rates of his players are what matters, but he'll know differently if the sole focus of his contract extension talks or the decision to fire him is his win-loss record."[321]

No matter what the disciplinary scheme or potential incentives a company decides to adopt, DOJ and SEC will consider whether they are fairly and consistently applied across the organization. No executive should be above compliance, no employee below compliance, and no person within an organization deemed too valuable to be disciplined, if warranted. Rewarding good behavior and sanctioning bad behavior reinforces a culture of compliance and ethics throughout an organization.

Third-Party Due Diligence and Payments

DOJ's and SEC's FCPA enforcement actions demonstrate that third parties, including agents, consultants, and distributors, are commonly used to conceal the payment of bribes to foreign officials in international business transactions. Risk-based due diligence is particularly important with third

---

321. Stephen M. Cutler, Director, Division of Enforcement, SEC, *Tone at the Top: Getting It Right,* Second Annual General Counsel Roundtable (Dec. 3, 2004), *available at* http://www.sec.gov/news/speech/spch120304smc.htm.

parties and will also be considered by DOJ and SEC in assessing the effectiveness of a company's compliance program.

Although the degree of appropriate due diligence may vary based on industry, country, size and nature of the transaction, and historical relationship with the third-party, some guiding principles always apply.

First, as part of risk-based due diligence, companies should understand the qualifications and associations of its third-party partners, including its business reputation, and relationship, if any, with foreign officials. The degree of scrutiny should increase as red flags surface.

Second, companies should have an understanding of the business rationale for including the third party in the transaction. Among other things, the company should understand the role of and need of the third party and ensure that the contract terms specifically describe the services to be performed. Additional considerations include payment terms and how those payment terms compare to typical terms in that industry and country, as well as the timing of the third party's introduction to the business. Moreover, companies may want to confirm and document that the third party is actually performing the work for which it is being paid and that its compensation is commensurate with the work being provided.

Third, companies should undertake some form of ongoing monitoring of third-party relationships.[322] Where appropriate, this may include updating due diligence periodically, exercising audit rights, providing periodic training, and requesting annual compliance certifications by the third party.

In addition to considering a company's due diligence on third parties, DOJ and SEC also assess whether the company has informed third parties of the company's compliance program and commitment to ethical and lawful business practices, and where appropriate, whether it has sought assurances from third parties, through certifications and otherwise, of reciprocal commitments. These can be meaningful ways to mitigate third-party risk.

Confidential Reporting and Internal Investigation

An effective compliance program should include a mechanism for an organization's employees and others to report suspected or actual misconduct or

---

322. *See, e.g.,* ICC Rules on Combating Corruption, *supra* note 309, at 8.

violations of the company's policies on a confidential basis and without fear of retaliation.[323] Companies may employ, for example, anonymous hotlines or ombudsmen. Moreover, once an allegation is made, companies should have in place an efficient, reliable, and properly funded process for investigating the allegation and documenting the company's response, including any disciplinary or remediation measures taken. Companies will want to consider taking "lessons learned" from any reported violations and the outcome of any resulting investigation to update their internal controls and compliance program and focus future training on such issues, as appropriate.

Continuous Improvement: Periodic Testing and Review

Finally, a good compliance program should constantly evolve. A company's business changes over time, as do the environments in which it operates, the nature of its customers, the laws that govern its actions, and the standards of its industry. In addition, compliance programs that do not just exist on paper but are followed in practice will inevitably uncover compliance weaknesses and require enhancements. Consequently, DOJ and SEC evaluate whether companies regularly review and improve their compliance programs and not allow them to become stale.

According to one survey, 64% of general counsel whose companies are subject to the FCPA say there is room for improvement in their FCPA training and compliance programs.[324] An organization should take the time to review and test its controls, and it should think critically about its potential weaknesses and risk areas. For example, some companies have undertaken employee surveys to measure their compliance culture and strength of internal controls, identify best practices, and detect new risk areas. Other companies periodically test their internal controls with targeted audits to make certain that controls on paper are working in practice. DOJ and SEC will give meaningful credit to thoughtful efforts to create a

---

323. *See, e.g.*, U.S. Sentencing Guidelines § 8B2.1(b)(5)(C); Compliance 101, *supra* note 302, at 30-33.

324. Corporate Board Member/FTI Consulting 2009 Legal Study, *Buckle Up. Boards and General Counsel May Face a Bumpy Ride in 2009,* at 5 ("Interestingly, while 67% of general counsel say their company is subject to compliance under the FCPA, 64% of those say there is room for improvement in their FCPA training and compliance programs.").

sustainable compliance program if a problem is later discovered. Similarly, undertaking proactive evaluations before a problem strikes can lower the applicable penalty range under the U.S. Sentencing Guidelines.[325] Although the nature and frequency of proactive evaluations may vary depending on the size and complexity of an organization, the idea behind such efforts is the same: continuous improvement and sustainability.[326]

Mergers and Acquisitions: Pre-Acquisition Due Diligence and Post-Acquisition Integration

In the context of the FCPA, mergers and acquisitions present both risks and opportunities. A company that does not perform adequate FCPA due diligence prior to a merger or acquisition may face both legal and business risks.[327] Perhaps most commonly, inadequate due diligence can allow a course of bribery to continue—with all the attendant harms to a business's profitability and reputation, as well as potential civil and criminal liability.

In contrast, companies that conduct effective FCPA due diligence on their acquisition targets are able to evaluate more accurately each target's value and negotiate for the costs of the bribery to be borne by the target. In addition, such actions demonstrate to DOJ and SEC a company's commitment to compliance and are taken into account when evaluating any potential enforcement action. For example, DOJ and SEC declined to take enforcement action against an acquiring issuer when the issuer, among other things, uncovered the corruption at the company being acquired as part of due diligence, ensured that the corruption was voluntarily disclosed to the government, cooperated with the investigation, and incorporated the acquired company into its compliance program and internal controls. On the other hand, SEC took action against the acquired company, and DOJ

---

325. *See*, U.S. SENTENCING GUIDELINES § 8B2.1(b)(5)(B) ("The organization shall take reasonable steps . . . to evaluate periodically the effectiveness of the organization's compliance and ethics program.").

326. *See, e.g.*, COMPLIANCE 101, *supra* note 302, at 60-61; THE ETHICS AND COMPLIANCE HANDBOOK, *supra* note 317, at 155-60; BUSINESS PRINCIPLES FOR COUNTERING, *supra* note 309, at 14.

327. *See, e.g.*, Michael M. Mannix and David S. Black, *Compliance Issues in M&A: Performing Due Diligence on the Target's Ethics and Compliance Program* at 5.71-5.81, *in* SOCIETY OF CORPORATE COMPLIANCE AND ETHICS, THE COMPLETE COMPLIANCE AND ETHICS MANUAL (2011).

took action against a subsidiary of the acquired company.[328] When pre-acquisition due diligence is not possible, DOJ has described procedures, contained in Opinion Procedure Release No. 08–02, pursuant to which companies can nevertheless be rewarded if they choose to conduct thorough post-acquisition FCPA due diligence.[329]

FCPA due diligence, however, is normally only a portion of the compliance process for mergers and acquisitions. DOJ and SEC evaluate whether the acquiring company promptly incorporated the acquired company into all of its internal controls, including its compliance program. Companies should consider training new employees, reevaluating third parties under company standards, and, where appropriate, conducting audits on new business units.

For example, as a result of due diligence conducted by a California-based issuer before acquiring the majority interest in a joint venture, the issuer learned of corrupt payments to obtain business. However, the issuer only implemented its internal controls "halfway" so as not to "choke the sales engine and cause a distraction for the sales guys." As a result, the improper payments continued, and the issuer was held liable for violating the FCPA's internal controls and books and records provisions.[330]

Other Guidance on Compliance and International Best Practices

In addition to this guide, the U.S. Departments of Commerce and State have both issued publications that contain guidance regarding compliance programs. The Department of Commerce's International Trade Administration has published *Business Ethics: A Manual for Managing a Responsible*

---

328. Complaint, SEC v. Syncor Int'l Corp., [No. 02-cv-2421 (D.D.C. Dec. 10, 2002), ECF No. 1, *available at* http://www.sec.gov/litigation/complaints/comp17887.htm]; Criminal Information, United States v. Syncor Taiwan, Inc., [No. 02-cr-1244 (C.D. Cal. Dec. 5, 2002), ECF No. 1, *available at* http://www.justice.gov/criminal/fraud/fcpa/cases/cyncor-taiwan/12-05-02syncor-taiwan-info.pdf].

329. U.S. DEPT. OF JUSTICE, FCPA OP. RELEASE 08-02 (June 13, 2008), *available at* http://justice.gov/criminal/fraud/fcpa/opinion/2008/0802.pdf.

330. Complaint, SEC v. Rae Sys., [Inc., No. 10-cv-2093 (D.D.C. Dec. 10, 2010), ECF No. 1, *available at* http://www.sec.gov/litigation/complaints/2010/comp21770.pdf]; Non-Pros. Agreement, *In re* Rae Sys. Inc. [(Dec. 10, 2010), *available at* http://www.justice.gov/criminal/fraud/fcpa/cases/rae-systems/12-10-10rae-systems.pdf].

Business Enterprises in Emerging Market Economies,[331] and the Department of State has published *Fighting Global Corruption: Business Risk Management.*[332]

There is also an emerging international consensus on compliance best practices, and a number of inter-governmental and non-governmental organizations have issued guidance regarding best practices for compliance.[333] Most notably, the OECD's 2009 Anti-Bribery Recommendation and its Annex II, *Good Practice Guidance on Internal Controls, Ethics, and Compliance,*[334] published in February 2010, were drafted based on consultations with the private sector and civil society and set forth specific good practices for ensuring effective compliance programs and measures for preventing and detecting foreign bribery. In addition, businesses may wish to refer to the following resources:

- Asia-Pacific Economic Cooperation – Anti-Corruption Code of Conduct for Businesses;[335]
- International Chamber of Commerce – ICC Rules on Combating Corruption;[336]
- Transparency International – Business Principles for Countering Bribery;[337]
- United Nations Global Compact – The Ten Principles;[338]
- World Bank – Integrity Compliance Guidelines;[339] and
- World Economic Forum – Partnering Against Corruption – Principles for Countering Bribery.[340]

---

331. U.S. DEPT. OF COMMERCE, BUSINESS ETHICS: A MANUAL FOR MANAGING A RESPONSIBLE BUSINESS ENTERPRISE IN EMERGING MARKET ECONOMIES (2004), *available at* http://www.ita.doc.gov/goodgovernance/adobe/bem_manual.pdf.

332. U.S. DEPT. OF STATE, FIGHTING GLOBAL CORRUPTION: BUSINESS RISK MANAGEMENT (2d ed. 2001), *available at* http://www.ogc.doc.gov/pdfs/Fighting_Global_Corruption.pdf.

333. *See* HARMONISING ANTI-CORRUPTION COMPLIANCE, *supra* note 302, at 46 ("Anti-corruption compliance is becoming more and more harmonised worldwide.").

334. OECD GOOD PRACTICE GUIDANCE, *supra* note 309.

335. APEC ANTI-CORRUPTION CODE, *supra* note 309.

336. ICC RULES ON COMBATING CORRUPTION, *supra* note 309.

337. BUSINESS PRINCIPLES FOR COUNTERING BRIBERY, *supra* note 309.

338. THE TEN PRINCIPLES, *supra* note 309.

339. INTEGRITY COMPLIANCE GUIDELINES, *supra* note 309.

340. PARTNERING AGAINST CORRUPTION, *supra* note 309.

Compliance Program Case Study

Recent DOJ and SEC actions relating to a financial institution's real estate transactions with a government agency in China illustrate the benefits of implementing and enforcing a comprehensive risk-based compliance program. The case involved a joint venture real estate investment in the Luwan District of Shanghai, China, between a U.S.-based financial institution and a state-owned entity that functioned as the District's real estate arm. The government entity conducted the transactions through two special purpose vehicles ("SPVs"), with the second SPV purchasing a 12% stake in a real estate project.

The financial institution, through a robust compliance program, frequently trained its employees, imposed a comprehensive payment-approval process designed to prevent bribery, and staffed a compliance department with a direct reporting line to the board of directors. As appropriate given the industry, market, and size and structure of the transactions, the financial institution (1) provided extensive FCPA training to the senior executive responsible for the transactions and (2) conducted extensive due diligence on the transactions, the local government entity, and the SPVs. Due diligence on the entity included reviewing Chinese government records; speaking with sources familiar with the Shanghai real estate market; checking the government entity's payment records and credit references; conducting an on-site visit and placing a pretextual telephone call to the entity's offices; searching media sources; and conducting background checks on the entity's principals. The financial institution vetted the SPVs by obtaining a letter with designated bank account information from a Chinese official associated with the government entity (the "Chinese Official"); using an international law firm to request and review 50 documents from the SPVs' Canadian attorney; interviewing the attorney; and interviewing the SPVs' management.

Notwithstanding the financial institution's robust compliance program and good faith enforcement of it, the company failed to learn that the Chinese Official personally owned nearly 50% of the second SPV (and therefore a nearly 6% stake in the joint venture) and that the SPV was used as a vehicle for corrupt payments. This failure was due, in large part, to misrepresentations by the Chinese Official, the financial institution's executive in charge of the project, and the SPV's attorney that the SPV was 100%

owned and controlled by the government entity. DOJ and SEC declined to take enforcement action against the financial institution, and its executive pleaded guilty to conspiracy to violate the FCPA's internal control provisions and also settled with SEC.

Hypothetical: Third-Party Vetting
Part 1:

Company A, a U.S. issuer headquartered in Delaware, wants to start doing business in a country that poses high risks of corruption. Company A learns about a potential $50 million contract with the country's Ministry of Immigration. This is a very attractive opportunity to Company A, both for its profitability and to open the door to future projects with the government. At the suggestion of the company's senior vice president of international sales (Sales Executive), Company A hires a local businessman who assures them he has strong ties to political and government leaders in a country and can help them win the contract. Company A enters into a consulting contract with the local businessman (Consultant). The agreement requires Consultant to use his best efforts to help the company win the business and provides for Consultant to receive a significant monthly retainer as well as a success fee of 3% of the value of any contract the company wins.

WHAT STEPS SHOULD COMPANY A CONSIDER
TAKING BEFORE HIRING CONSULTANT?

There are several factors here that might lead Company A to perform FCPA-related due diligence prior to retaining Consultant: (1) the market (high-risk country); (2) the size and significance of the deal to the company; (3) the company's first time use of this particular consultant; (4) the consultant's strong ties to political and government leaders; (5) the success fee structure of the contract; and (6) the vaguely-defined services to be provided. In order to minimize the likelihood of incurring FCPA liability, Company A should carefully vet Consultant and his role in the transaction, including close scrutiny of the relationship between Consultant and any Ministry of Immigration officials or other government officials. Although there is nothing inherently illegal about contracting with a third party that has close connections to politicians and government officials to perform legitimate services on a transaction, this type of relationship can be susceptible to corruption. Among other things, Company A may consider conducting due diligence on Consultant, including background and reference checks; ensuring that the contract spells out exactly what services and deliverables (such as written status reports or other documentation) Consultant is providing; training Consultant on the FCPA and other anti-corruption laws; requiring Consultant to represent that he will abide by the FCPA and other anti-corruption laws; including audit rights in the contract (and exercising those rights); and ensuring that payments requested by Consultant have the proper supporting documentation before they are approved for payment.

Part 2: Distributors and Local Partners
ASSUME THE FOLLOWING ALTERNATIVE FACTS:

Instead of hiring Consultant, Company A retains an often-used local distributor (Distributor) to sell Company A's products to the Ministry of Immigration. In negotiating the price structure, Distributor, which had introduced the project to Company A, claims that the standard discount price to Distributor creates insufficient margin for Distributor to cover warehousing, distribution, installation, marketing, and training costs and requests an additional discount or rebate, or, in the alternative, a contribution to its marketing efforts, either in the form of a lump sum or as a percentage of the total contract. This requested discount/allowance is significantly larger than usual, although there is precedent at Company A for granting this level of discount in unique circumstances. Distributor further advises Company A that the Ministry's procurement officials responsible for awarding the contract have expressed a strong preference for including a particular local company (Local Partner) in the transaction as a subcontractor of Company A to perform installation, training, and other services that would normally have been performed by Distributor or Company A. According to Distributor, the Ministry has a solid working relationship with Local Partner, and it would cause less disruption for Local Partner to perform most of the on-site work at the Ministry. One of the principals (Principal 1) of the Local Partner is an official in another government ministry.

WHAT ADDITIONAL COMPLIANCE CONSIDERATIONS
DO THESE ALTERNATIVE FACTS RAISE?

As with Consultant in the first scenario above, Company A should carefully vet Distributor and Local Partner and their roles in the transaction in order to minimize the likelihood of incurring FCPA liability. While Company A has an established relationship with Distributor, the fact that Distributor has requested an additional discount warrants further inquiry into the economic justification for the change, particularly where, as here, the proposed transaction structure contemplates paying Local Partner to provide many of the same services that Distributor would otherwise provide. In many cases, it may be appropriate for distributors to receive larger discounts to account for unique circumstances in particular transactions. That said, a common mechanism to create additional margin for bribe payments is through excessive discounts or rebates to distributors. Accordingly, when a company has pre-existing relationships with distributors and other third parties, transaction-specific due diligence—including an analysis of payment terms to confirm that the payment is commensurate with the work being performed—can be critical even in circumstances where due diligence of the distributor or other third party raises no initial red flags.

Company A should carefully scrutinize the relationship among Local Partner, Distributor, and Ministry of Immigration officials. While there is nothing inherently illegal about contracting with a third party that is recommended by the end-user, or even hiring a government official to perform legitimate services on a transaction unrelated to his or her government job, these facts raise additional red flags that warrant significant scrutiny. Among other things, Company A would be well-advised to require Principal 1 to verify that he will have no role in the Ministry of Immigration's decision to award the contract to Company A, notify the Ministry of Immigration and his own ministry of his proposed involvement in the transaction, and certify that he will abide by the FCPA and other anti-corruption laws and that his involvement in the transaction is permitted under local law.

ASSUME THE FOLLOWING ADDITIONAL FACTS:

Under its company policy for a government transaction of this size, Company A requires both finance and compliance approval. The finance officer is concerned that the discounts to Distributor are significantly larger than what they have approved for similar work and will cut too deeply into Company A's profit margin. The finance officer is also skeptical about including Local Partner to perform some of the same services that Company A is paying Distributor to perform. Unsatisfied with Sales Executive's explanation, she requests a meeting with Distributor and Principal 1. At the meeting, Distributor and Principal 1 offer vague and inconsistent justifications for the payments and fail to provide any supporting analysis, and Principal 1 seems to have no real expertise in the industry. During a coffee break, Distributor comments to Sales Executive that the finance officer is naïve about "how business is done in my country." Following the meeting, Sales Executive dismisses the finance officer's concerns, assuring her that the proposed transaction structure is reasonable and legitimate. Sales Executive also reminds the finance officer that "the deal is key to their growth in the industry."

The compliance officer focuses his due diligence on vetting Distributor and Local Partner and hires a business investigative firm to conduct a background check. Distributor appears reputable, capable, and financially stable and is willing to take on real risk in the project, financial and otherwise. However, the compliance officer learns that Distributor has established an off-shore bank account for the transaction. The compliance officer further learns that Local Partner's business was organized two years ago and appears financially stable but has no expertise in the industry and has established an off-shore shell company and bank account to conduct this transaction. The background check also reveals that Principal 1 is a former college roommate of a senior official of the Ministry of Immigration. The Sales Executive dismisses the compliance officer's concerns, commenting that what Local Partner does with its payments "isn't our problem." Sales Executive also strongly objects to the compliance officer's request to meet with Principal 1 to discuss the off-shore company and account, assuring him that it was done for legitimate tax purposes and complaining that if Company A continues to "harass" Local Partner and Distributor, they would partner with Company A's chief competitor. The compliance officer and the finance officer discuss their concerns with each other but ultimately sign off on the deal even though their questions had not been answered. Their decision is motivated in large part by their conversation with Sales

Executive, who told them that this was the region's most important contract and that the detailed FCPA questionnaires and robust anti-corruption representation in the contracts placed the burden on Distributor and Local Partner to act ethically.

Company A goes forward with the Distributor and Local Partner agreements and wins the contract after six months. The finance officer approves Company A's payments to Local Partner via the offshore account, even though Local Partner's invoices did not contain supporting detail or documentation of any services provided. Company A recorded the payments as legitimate operational expenses on its books and records. Sales Executive received a large year-end bonus due to the award of the contract.

In fact, Local Partner and Distributor used part of the payments and discount margin, respectively, to funnel bribe payments to several Ministry of Immigration officials, including Principal 1's former college roommate, in exchange for awarding the contract to Company A. Thousands of dollars are also wired to the personal offshore bank account of Sales Executive.

HOW WOULD DOJ AND SEC EVALUATE THE POTENTIAL
FCPA LIABILITY OF COMPANY A AND ITS EMPLOYEES?
This is not the case of a single "rogue employee" circumventing an otherwise robust compliance program. Although Company A's finance and compliance officers had the correct instincts to scrutinize the structure and economics of the transaction and the role of the third parties, their due diligence was incomplete. When the initial inquiry identified significant red flags, they approved the transaction despite knowing that their concerns were unanswered or the answers they received raised additional concerns and red flags. Relying on due diligence questionnaires and anti-corruption representations is insufficient, particularly when the risks are readily apparent. Nor can Company A or its employees shield themselves from liability because it was Distributor and Local Partner—rather than Company A directly—that made the payments.

The facts suggest that Sales Executive had actual knowledge of or was willfully blind to the consultant's payment of the bribes. He also personally profited from the scheme (both from the kickback and from the bonus he received from the company) and intentionally discouraged the finance and compliance officers from learning the full story. Sales Executive is therefore subject to liability under the anti-bribery, books and records, and internal controls provision of the FCPA, and others may be as well. Company A may also be liable for violations of the anti-bribery, books and records, and internal controls provisions of the FCPA given the number and significance of red flags that established a high probability of bribery and the role of employees and agents acting on the company's behalf.

Appendix B

Excerpt - The Bribery Act 2010: Guidance about procedures which relevant commercial organisations can put into place to prevent persons associated with them from bribing (section 9 of the Bribery Act 2010) ('Government Guidance')**

* * *

The Six Principles

The Government considers that procedures put in place by commercial organisations wishing to prevent bribery being committed on their behalf should be informed by six principles. These are set out below. Commentary and guidance on what procedures the application of the principles may produce accompanies each principle.

** Ministry of Justice, The Bribery Act 2010: Guidance about procedures which relevant commercial organisations can put in place to prevent persons associated with them from bribery (2011), *available at* http://www.justice.gov.uk/downloads/legislation/bribery-act-2010-guidance.pdf.

These principles are not prescriptive. They are intended to be flexible and outcome focussed, allowing for the huge variety of circumstances that commercial organisations find themselves in. Small organisations will, for example, face different challenges to those faced by large multi-national enterprises. Accordingly, the detail of how organisations might apply these principles, taken as a whole, will vary, but the outcome should always be robust and effective anti-bribery procedures.

As set out in more detail below, bribery prevention procedures should be proportionate to risk. Although commercial organisations with entirely domestic operations may require bribery prevention procedures, we believe that as a general proposition they will face lower risks of bribery on their behalf by associated persons than the risks that operate in foreign markets. In any event procedures put in place to mitigate domestic bribery risks are likely to be similar if not the same as those designed to mitigate those associated with foreign markets.

A series of case studies based on hypothetical scenarios is provided at [the end]. These are designed to illustrate the application of the principles for small, medium and large organisations.

Principle 1
Proportionate Procedures

A commercial organisation's procedures to prevent bribery by persons associated with it are proportionate to the bribery risks it faces and to the nature, scale and complexity of the commercial organisation's activities. They are also clear, practical, accessible, effectively implemented and enforced.

Commentary

1.1   The term 'procedures' is used in this guidance to embrace both bribery prevention policies and the procedures which implement them. Policies articulate a commercial organisation's anti-bribery stance, show how it will be maintained and help to create an anti-bribery culture. They are therefore a necessary measure in the prevention of bribery, but they will not achieve that objective unless they are properly implemented. Further guidance on implementation is provided through principles 2 to 6.

1.2   Adequate bribery prevention procedures ought to be proportionate to the bribery risks that the organisation faces. An initial assessment of risk across the organisation is therefore a necessary first step. To a certain extent the level of risk will be linked to the size of the organisation and the nature and complexity of its business, but size will not be the only determining factor. Some small organisations can face quite significant risks, and will need more extensive procedures than their counterparts facing limited risks. However, small organisations are unlikely to need procedures that are as extensive as those of a large multi-national organisation. For example, a very small business may be able to rely heavily on periodic oral briefings to communicate its policies while a large one may need to rely on extensive written communication.

1.3   The level of risk that organisations face will also vary with the type and nature of the persons associated with it. For example, a commercial organisation that properly assesses that there is no risk of bribery on the part of one of its associated persons will accordingly require nothing in the way of procedures to prevent bribery in the context of that relationship. By the same token the bribery risks associated with reliance on a third party agent representing a commercial organisation in negotiations with foreign public officials may be assessed as significant and accordingly require much more in the way of procedures to mitigate those risks. Organisations are likely to need to select procedures to cover a broad range of risks but any consideration by a court in an individual case of the adequacy of procedures is likely necessarily to focus on those procedures designed to prevent bribery on the part of the associated person committing the offence in question.

1.4   Bribery prevention procedures may be stand alone or form part of wider guidance, for example on recruitment or on managing a tender process in public procurement. Whatever the chosen model, the procedures should seek to ensure there is a practical and realistic means of achieving the organisation's stated anti-bribery policy objectives across all of the organisation's functions.

1.5   The Government recognises that applying these procedures retrospectively to existing associated persons is more difficult, but this should be done over time, adopting a risk-based approach and with due allowance for what is practicable and the level of control over existing arrangements.

Procedures

1.6   Commercial organisations' bribery prevention policies are likely to include certain common elements. As an indicative and not exhaustive list, an organisation may wish to cover in its policies:

- its commitment to bribery prevention (see Principle 2)
- its general approach to mitigation of specific bribery risks, such as those arising from the conduct of intermediaries and agents, or those associated with hospitality and promotional expenditure, facilitation payments or political and charitable donations or contributions; (see Principle 3 on risk assessment)
- an overview of its strategy to implement its bribery prevention policies.

1.7   The procedures put in place to implement an organisation's bribery prevention policies should be designed to mitigate identified risks as well as to prevent deliberate unethical conduct on the part of associated persons. The following is an indicative and not exhaustive list of the topics that bribery prevention procedures might embrace depending on the particular risks faced:

- The involvement of the organisation's top-level management (see Principle 2).
- Risk assessment procedures (see Principle 3).
- Due diligence of existing or prospective associated persons (see Principle 4).
- The provision of gifts, hospitality and promotional expenditure; charitable and political donations; or demands for facilitation payments.
- Direct and indirect employment, including recruitment, terms and conditions, disciplinary action and remuneration.
- Governance of business relationships with all other associated persons including pre and post contractual agreements.
- Financial and commercial controls such as adequate bookkeeping, auditing and approval of expenditure.
- Transparency of transactions and disclosure of information.
- Decision making, such as delegation of authority procedures, separation of functions and the avoidance of conflicts of interest.
- Enforcement, detailing discipline processes and sanctions for breaches of the organisation's anti-bribery rules.
- The reporting of bribery including 'speak up' or 'whistle blowing' procedures.
- The detail of the process by which the organisation plans to implement its bribery prevention procedures, for example, how its policy will be applied to individual projects and to different parts of the organisation.
- The communication of the organisation's policies and procedures, and training in their application (see Principle 5). The monitoring, review and evaluation of bribery prevention procedures (see Principle 6).

Principle 2
Top-Level Commitment

The top-level management of a commercial organisation (be it a board of directors, the owners or any other equivalent body or person) are committed to preventing bribery by persons associated with it. They foster a culture within the organisation in which bribery is never acceptable.

Commentary

2.1   Those at the top of an organisation are in the best position to foster a culture of integrity where bribery is unacceptable. The purpose of this principle is to encourage the involvement of top-level management in the determination of bribery prevention procedures. It is also to encourage top-level involvement in any key decision making relating to bribery risk where that is appropriate for the organisation's management structure.

Procedures

2.2   Whatever the size, structure or market of a commercial organisation, top-level management commitment to bribery prevention is likely to include (1) communication of the organisation's anti-bribery stance, and (2) an appropriate degree of involvement in developing bribery prevention procedures.

Internal and External Communication of the Commitment to Zero Tolerance to Bribery

2.3   This could take a variety of forms. A formal statement appropriately communicated can be very effective in establishing an anti-bribery culture within an organisation. Communication might be tailored to different audiences. The statement would probably need to be drawn to people's attention on a periodic basis and could be generally available, for example on an organisation's intranet and/or internet site. Effective formal statements that demonstrate top level commitment are likely to include:

- a commitment to carry out business fairly, honestly and openly
- a commitment to zero tolerance towards bribery
- the consequences of breaching the policy for employees and managers
- for other associated persons the consequences of breaching contractual provisions relating to bribery prevention (this could include a reference to avoiding doing business with others who do not commit to doing business without bribery as a 'best practice' objective)
- articulation of the business benefits of rejecting bribery (reputational, customer and business partner confidence)
- reference to the range of bribery prevention procedures the commercial organization has or is putting in place, including any protection and procedures for confidential reporting of bribery (whistle-blowing)
- key individuals and departments involved in the development and implementation of the organisation's bribery prevention procedures
- reference to the organisation's involvement in any collective action against bribery in, for example, the same business sector.

Top-Level Involvement in Bribery Prevention

2.4   Effective leadership in bribery prevention will take a variety of forms appropriate for and proportionate to the organisation's size, management structure and circumstances. In smaller organisations a proportionate response may require top-level managers to be personally involved in initiating, developing and implementing bribery prevention procedures and bribery critical decision making. In a large multi-national organisation the board should be responsible for setting bribery prevention policies, tasking management to design, operate and monitor bribery prevention procedures, and keeping these policies and procedures under regular review. But whatever the appropriate model, top-level engagement is likely to reflect the following elements:

- Selection and training of senior managers to lead anti-bribery work where appropriate.
- Leadership on key measures such as a code of conduct.
- Endorsement of all bribery prevention related publications.
- Leadership in awareness raising and encouraging transparent dialogue throughout the organisation so as to seek to ensure effective dissemination of anti-bribery policies and procedures to employees, subsidiaries, and associated persons, etc.
- Engagement with relevant associated persons and external bodies, such as sectoral organizations and the media, to help articulate the organisation's policies.
- Specific involvement in high profile and critical decision making where appropriate.
- Assurance of risk assessment.
- General oversight of breaches of procedures and the provision of feedback to the board or equivalent, where appropriate, on levels of compliance.

Principle 3
Risk Assessment
The commercial organisation assesses the nature and extent of its exposure to potential external and internal risks of bribery on its behalf by persons associated with it. The assessment is periodic, informed and documented.

Commentary

3.1   For many commercial organisations this principle will manifest itself as part of a more general risk assessment carried out in relation to business objectives. For others, its application may produce a more specific stand alone bribery risk assessment. The purpose of this principle is to promote the adoption of risk assessment procedures that are proportionate to the organisation's size and structure and to the nature, scale and location of its activities. But whatever approach is adopted the fuller the understanding of the bribery risks an organisation faces the more effective its efforts to prevent bribery are likely to be.

3.2 Some aspects of risk assessment involve procedures that fall within the generally accepted meaning of the term 'due diligence'. The role of due diligence as a risk mitigation tool is separately dealt with under Principle 4.

Procedures

3.3 Risk assessment procedures that enable the commercial organisation accurately to identify and prioritise the risks it faces will, whatever its size, activities, customers or markets, usually reflect a few basic characteristics. These are:

- Oversight of the risk assessment by top level management.
- Appropriate resourcing—this should reflect the scale of the organisation's business and the need to identify and prioritise all relevant risks.
- Identification of the internal and external information sources that will enable risk to be assessed and reviewed.
- Due diligence enquiries (see Principle 4).
- Accurate and appropriate documentation of the risk assessment and its conclusions.

3.4 As a commercial organisation's business evolves, so will the bribery risks it faces and hence so should its risk assessment. For example, the risk assessment that applies to a commercial organisation's domestic operations might not apply when it enters a new market in a part of the world in which it has not done business before (see Principle 6 for more on this).

Commonly encountered risks

3.5 Commonly encountered external risks can be categorised into five broad groups—country, sectoral, transaction, business opportunity and business partnership:

- *Country risk:* this is evidenced by perceived high levels of corruption, an absence of effectively implemented anti-bribery legislation and a failure of the foreign government, media, local business community and civil society effectively to promote transparent procurement and investment policies.
- *Sectoral risk:* some sectors are higher risk than others. Higher risk sectors include the extractive industries and the large scale infrastructure sector.
- *Transaction risk:* certain types of transaction give rise to higher risks, for example, charitable or political contributions, licences and permits, and transactions relating to public procurement.
- *Business opportunity risk:* such risks might arise in high value projects or with projects involving many contractors or intermediaries; or with projects which are not apparently undertaken at market prices, or which do not have a clear legitimate objective.
- *Business partnership risk:* certain relationships may involve higher risk, for example, the use of intermediaries in transactions with foreign public officials; consortia or joint venture partners; and relationships with politically exposed persons where the proposed

business relationship involves, or is linked to, a prominent public official.

3.6   An assessment of external bribery risks is intended to help decide how those risks can be mitigated by procedures governing the relevant operations or business relationships; but a bribery risk assessment should also examine the extent to which internal structures or procedures may themselves add to the level of risk. Commonly encountered internal factors may include:

- deficiencies in employee training, skills and knowledge
- bonus culture that rewards excessive risk taking
- lack of clarity in the organisation's policies on, and procedures for, hospitality and promotional expenditure, and political or charitable contributions
- lack of clear financial controls
- lack of a clear anti-bribery message from the top-level management.

Principle 4
Due Diligence

The commercial organisation applies due diligence procedures, taking a proportionate and risk based approach, in respect of persons who perform or will perform services for or on behalf of the organisation, in order to mitigate identified bribery risks.

Commentary

4.1   Due diligence is firmly established as an element of corporate good governance and it is envisaged that due diligence related to bribery prevention will often form part of a wider due diligence framework. Due diligence procedures are both a form of bribery risk assessment (see Principle 3) and a means of mitigating a risk. By way of illustration, a commercial organisation may identify risks that as a general proposition attach to doing business in reliance upon local third party intermediaries. Due diligence of specific prospective third party intermediaries could significantly mitigate these risks. The significance of the role of due diligence in bribery risk mitigation justifies its inclusion here as a Principle in its own right.

4.2   The purpose of this Principle is to encourage commercial organisations to put in place due diligence procedures that adequately inform the application of proportionate measures designed to prevent persons associated with them from bribing on their behalf.

Procedures

4.3   As this guidance emphasises throughout, due diligence procedures should be proportionate to the identified risk. They can also be undertaken internally or by external consultants. A person 'associated' with a commercial organisation as set out at section 8 of the Bribery Act includes any person performing services for a commercial organisation. As explained at paragraphs 37 to 43 in the section 'Government Policy and section 7', the scope of this definition is broad and can embrace a wide range of business relationships. But the appropriate level of due diligence to prevent bribery will vary enormously depending on the risks arising from the particular relationship. So, for example, the appropriate level of due diligence required by a commercial organisation when contracting for the performance of information technology services may be low, to reflect low risks of bribery on its behalf. In contrast, an organisation that is selecting an intermediary to assist in establishing a business in foreign markets will typically require a much higher level of due diligence to mitigate the risks of bribery on its behalf.

4.4   Organisations will need to take considerable care in entering into certain business relationships, due to the particular circumstances in which the relationships come into existence. An example is where local law or convention dictates the use of local agents in circumstances where it may be difficult for a commercial organisation to extricate itself from a business relationship once established. The importance of thorough due diligence and risk mitigation prior to any commitment are paramount in such circumstances. Another relationship that carries particularly important due diligence implications is a merger of commercial organisations or an acquisition of one by another.

4.5   'Due diligence' for the purposes of Principle 4 should be conducted using a risk-based approach (as referred to on page 27). For example, in lower risk situations, commercial organisations may decide that there is no need to conduct much in the way of due diligence. In higher risk situations, due diligence may include conducting direct interrogative enquiries, indirect investigations, or general research on proposed associated persons. Appraisal and continued monitoring of recruited or engaged 'associated' persons may also be required, proportionate to the identified risks. Generally, more information is likely to be required from prospective and existing associated persons that are incorporated (e.g. companies) than from individuals. This is because on a basic level more individuals are likely to be involved in the performance of services by a company and the exact nature of the roles of such individuals or other connected bodies may not be immediately obvious. Accordingly, due diligence may involve direct requests for details on the background, expertise and business experience, of relevant individuals. This information can then be verified through research and the following up of references, etc.

4.6   A commercial organisation's employees are presumed to be persons 'associated' with the organisation for the purposes of the Bribery Act. The organisation may wish, therefore, to incorporate in its recruitment and human resources procedures an appropriate level of due diligence to mitigate the risks of bribery being undertaken by employees which is proportionate to the risk associated with the post in question. Due diligence is unlikely to be needed in relation to lower risk posts.

Principle 5
Communication (including training)

The commercial organisation seeks to ensure that its bribery prevention policies and procedures are embedded and understood throughout the organisation through internal and external communication, including training, that is proportionate to the risks it faces.

Commentary

5.1 Communication and training deters bribery by associated persons by enhancing awareness and understanding of a commercial organisation's procedures and to the organisation's commitment to their proper application. Making information available assists in more effective monitoring, evaluation and review of bribery prevention procedures. Training provides the knowledge and skills needed to employ the organisation's procedures and deal with any bribery related problems or issues that may arise.

Procedures
Communication

5.2 The content, language and tone of communications for internal consumption may vary from that for external use in response to the different relationship the audience has with the commercial organisation. The nature of communication will vary enormously between commercial organisations in accordance with the different bribery risks faced, the size of the organisation and the scale and nature of its activities.

5.3 Internal communications should convey the 'tone from the top' but are also likely to focus on the implementation of the organisation's policies and procedures and the implications for employees. Such communication includes policies on particular areas such as decision making, financial control, hospitality and promotional expenditure, facilitation payments, training, charitable and political donations and penalties for breach of rules and the articulation of management roles at different levels. Another important aspect of internal communications is the establishment of a secure, confidential and accessible means for internal or external parties to raise concerns about bribery on the part of associated persons, to provide suggestions for improvement of bribery prevention procedures and controls and for requesting advice. These so called 'speak up' procedures can amount to a very helpful management tool for commercial organisations with diverse operations that may be in many countries. If these procedures are to be effective there must be adequate protection for those reporting concerns.

5.4   External communication of bribery prevention policies through a statement or codes of conduct, for example, can reassure existing and prospective associated persons and can act as a deterrent to those intending to bribe on a commercial organisation's behalf. Such communications can include information on bribery prevention procedures and controls, sanctions, results of internal surveys, rules governing recruitment, procurement and tendering. A commercial organisation may consider it proportionate and appropriate to communicate its anti-bribery policies and commitment to them to a wider audience, such as other organisations in its sector and to sectoral organisations that would fall outside the scope of the range of its associated persons, or to the general public.

Training

5.5   Like all procedures training should be proportionate to risk but some training is likely to be effective in firmly establishing an anti-bribery culture whatever the level of risk. Training may take the form of education and awareness raising about the threats posed by bribery in general and in the sector or areas in which the organisation operates in particular, and the various ways it is being addressed.

5.6   General training could be mandatory for new employees or for agents (on a weighted risk basis) as part of an induction process, but it should also be tailored to the specific risks associated with specific posts. Consideration should also be given to tailoring training to the special needs of those involved in any 'speak up' procedures, and higher risk functions such as purchasing, contracting, distribution and marketing, and working in high risk countries. Effective training is continuous, and regularly monitored and evaluated.

5.7   It may be appropriate to require associated persons to undergo training. This will be particularly relevant for high risk associated persons. In any event, organisations may wish to encourage associated persons to adopt bribery prevention training.

5.8   Nowadays there are many different training formats available in addition to the traditional classroom or seminar formats, such as e-learning and other web-based tools. But whatever the format, the training ought to achieve its objective of ensuring that those participating in it develop a firm understanding of what the relevant policies and procedures mean in practice for them.

Principle 6
Monitoring and Review

The commercial organisation monitors and reviews procedures designed to prevent bribery by persons associated with it and makes improvements where necessary.

Commentary

6.1   The bribery risks that a commercial organisation faces may change over time, as may the nature and scale of its activities, so the procedures required to mitigate those risks are also likely to change. Commercial organisations will therefore wish to consider how to monitor and evaluate the effectiveness of their bribery prevention procedures and adapt them where necessary. In addition to regular monitoring, an organisation might want to review its processes in response to other stimuli, for example governmental changes in countries in which they operate, an incident of bribery or negative press reports.

Procedures

6.2   There is a wide range of internal and external review mechanisms which commercial organisations could consider using. Systems set up to deter, detect and investigate bribery, and monitor the ethical quality of transactions, such as internal financial control mechanisms, will help provide insight into the effectiveness of procedures designed to prevent bribery. Staff surveys, questionnaires and feedback from training can also provide an important source of information on effectiveness and a means by which employees and other associated persons can inform continuing improvement of anti-bribery policies.

6.3   Organisations could also consider formal periodic reviews and reports for top-level management. Organisations could also draw on information on other organisations' practices, for example relevant trade bodies or regulators might highlight examples of good or bad practice in their publications.

6.4   In addition, organisations might wish to consider seeking some form of external verification or assurance of the effectiveness of anti-bribery procedures. Some organisations may be able to apply for certified compliance with one of the independently-verified anti-bribery standards maintained by industrial sector associations or multilateral bodies. However, such certification may not necessarily mean that a commercial organisation's bribery prevention procedures are 'adequate' for all purposes where an offence under section 7 of the Bribery Act could be charged.

* * *

Bribery Act 2010 Case Studies

Introduction

These case studies (which do not form part of the guidance issued under section 9 of the Act) look at how the application of the six principles might relate to a number of hypothetical scenarios commercial organisations may encounter. The Government believes that this illustrative context can assist commercial organisations in deciding what procedures to prevent persons associated with them from bribing on their behalf might be most suitable to their needs.

These case studies are illustrative. They are intended to complement the guidance. They do not replace or supersede any of the principles. The considerations set out below merely show in some circumstances how the principles can be applied, and should not be seen as standard setting, establishing any presumption, reflecting a minimum baseline of action or being appropriate for all organisations whatever their size. Accordingly, the considerations set out below are not:

- comprehensive of all considerations in all circumstances
- conclusive of adequate procedures
- conclusive of inadequate procedures if not all of the considerations are considered and/or applied.

All but one of these case studies focus on bribery risks associated with foreign markets. This is because bribery risks associated with foreign markets are generally higher than those associated with domestic markets. Accordingly case studies focusing on foreign markets are better suited as vehicles for the illustration of bribery prevention procedures.

Case Study 1 – Principle 1
Facilitation payments
A medium sized company ('A') has acquired a new customer in a foreign country ('B') where it operates through its agent company ('C'). Its bribery risk assessment has identified facilitation payments as a significant problem in securing reliable importation into B and transport to its new customer's manufacturing locations. These sometimes take the form of 'inspection fees' required before B's import inspectors will issue a certificate of inspection and thereby facilitate the clearance of goods.

A could consider any or a combination of the following:

- Communication of its policy of non-payment of facilitation payments to C and its staff.
- Seeking advice on the law of B relating to certificates of inspection and fees for these to differentiate between properly payable fees and disguised requests for facilitation payments.
- Building realistic timescales into the planning of the project so that shipping, importation and delivery schedules allow where feasible for resisting and testing demands for facilitation payments.
- Requesting that C train its staff about resisting demands for facilitation payments and the relevant local law and provisions of the Bribery Act 2010.
- Proposing or including as part of any contractual arrangement certain procedures for C and its staff, which may include one or more of the following, if appropriate:
  - questioning of legitimacy of demands
  - requesting receipts and identification details of the official making the demand
  - requests to consult with superior officials
  - trying to avoid paying 'inspection fees' (if not properly due) in cash and directly to an official
  - informing those demanding payments that compliance with the demand may mean that A (and possibly C) will commit an offence under UK law

- informing those demanding payments that it will be necessary for C to inform the UK embassy of the demand.
- Maintaining close liaison with C so as to keep abreast of any local developments that may provide solutions and encouraging C to develop its own strategies based on local knowledge.
- Use of any UK diplomatic channels or participation in locally active non-governmental organisations, so as to apply pressure on the authorities of B to take action to stop demands for facilitation payments.

Case Study 2 – Principle 1
Proportionate procedures

A small to medium sized installation company is operating entirely within the United Kingdom domestic market. It relies to varying degrees on independent consultants to facilitate business opportunities and to assist in the preparation of both pre-qualification submissions and formal tenders in seeking new business. Such consultants work on an arms-length-fee-plus-expenses basis. They are engaged by sales staff and selected because of their extensive network of business contacts and the specialist information they have. The reason for engaging them is to enhance the company's prospects of being included in tender and pre-qualification lists and of being selected as main or sub-contractors. The reliance on consultants and, in particular, difficulties in monitoring expenditure which sometimes involves cash transactions has been identified by the company as a source of medium to high risk of bribery being undertaken on the company's behalf.

In seeking to mitigate these risks the company could consider any or a combination of the following:

- Communication of a policy statement committing it to transparency and zero tolerance of bribery in pursuit of its business objectives. The statement could be communicated to the company's employees, known consultants and external contacts, such as sectoral bodies and local chambers of commerce.
- Firming up its due diligence before engaging consultants. This could include making enquiries through business contacts, local chambers

of commerce, business associations, or internet searches and following up any business references and financial statements.

- Considering firming up the terms of the consultants' contracts so that they reflect a commitment to zero tolerance of bribery, set clear criteria for provision of bona fide hospitality on the company's behalf and define in detail the basis of remuneration, including expenses.
- Consider making consultants' contracts subject to periodic review and renewal.
- Drawing up key points guidance on preventing bribery for its sales staff and all other staff involved in bidding for business and when engaging consultants.
- Periodically emphasizing these policies and procedures at meetings – for example, this might form a standing item on meeting agendas every few months.
- Providing a confidential means for staff and external business contracts to air any suspicions of the use of bribery on the company's behalf.

Case Study 3 – Principles 1 and 6
Joint venture

A medium sized company ('D') is interested in significant foreign mineral deposits. D proposes to enter into a joint venture with a local mining company ('E'). It is proposed that D and E would have an equal holding in the joint venture company ('DE'). D identifies the necessary interaction between DE and local public officials as a source of significant risks of bribery.

D could consider negotiating for the inclusion of any or a combination of the following bribery prevention procedures into the agreement setting up DE:

- Parity of representation on the board of DE.
- That DE put in place measures designed to ensure compliance with all applicable bribery and corruption laws. These measures might cover such issues as:
  - gifts and hospitality
  - agreed decision making rules

- procurement
- engagement of third parties, including due diligence requirements
- conduct of relations with public officials
- training for staff in high risk positions
- record keeping and accounting.
- The establishment of an audit committee with at least one representative of each of D and E that has the power to view accounts and certain expenditure and prepare regular reports.
- Binding commitments by D and E to comply with all applicable bribery laws in relation to the operation of DE, with a breach by either D or E being a breach of the agreement between them. Where such a breach is a material breach this could lead to termination or other similarly significant consequences.

Case Study 4 – Principles 1 and 5
Hospitality and promotional expenditure

A firm of engineers ('F') maintains a programme of annual events providing entertainment, quality dining and attendance at various sporting occasions, as an expression of appreciation of its long association with its business partners. Private bodies and individuals are happy to meet their own travel and accommodation costs associated with attending these events. The costs of the travel and accommodation of any foreign public officials attending are, however, met by F.

F could consider any or a combination of the following:

- Conducting a bribery risk assessment relating to its dealings with business partners and foreign public officials and in particular the provision of hospitality and promotional expenditure.
- Publication of a policy statement committing it to transparent, proportionate, reasonable and bona fide hospitality and promotional expenditure.
- The issue of internal guidance on procedures that apply to the provision of hospitality and/or promotional expenditure providing:
  - that any procedures are designed to seek to ensure transparency and conformity with any relevant laws and codes applying to F

- that any procedures are designed to seek to ensure transparency and conformity with the relevant laws and codes applying to foreign public officials
- that any hospitality should reflect a desire to cement good relations and show appreciation, and that promotional expenditure should seek to improve the image of F as a commercial organisation, to better present its products or services, or establish cordial relations
- that the recipient should not be given the impression that they are under an obligation to confer any business advantage or that the recipient's independence will be affected
- criteria to be applied when deciding the appropriate levels of hospitality for both private and public business partners, clients, suppliers and foreign public officials and the type of hospitality that is appropriate in different sets of circumstances;
- that provision of hospitality for public officials be cleared with the relevant public body so that it is clear who and what the hospitality is for
- for expenditure over certain limits, approval by an appropriately senior level of management may be a relevant consideration
- accounting (book-keeping, orders, invoices, delivery notes, etc).
- Regular monitoring, review and evaluation of internal procedures and compliance with them.
- Appropriate training and supervision provided to staff.

Case Study 5 – Principle 3
Assessing risks
A small specialist manufacturer is seeking to expand its business in one of several emerging markets, all of which offer comparable opportunities. It has no specialist risk assessment expertise and is unsure how to go about assessing the risks of entering a new market.

The small manufacturer could consider any or a combination of the following:

- Incorporating an assessment of bribery risk into research to identify the optimum market for expansion.
- Seeking advice from UK diplomatic services and government organisations such as UK Trade and Investment.
- Consulting general country assessments undertaken by local chambers of commerce, relevant non-governmental organisations and sectoral organisations.
- Seeking advice from industry representatives.
- Following up any general or specialist advice with further independent research.

Case Study 6 – Principle 4
Due diligence of agents

A medium to large sized manufacturer of specialist equipment ('G') has an opportunity to enter an emerging market in a foreign country ('H') by way of a government contract to supply equipment to the state. Local convention requires any foreign commercial organisations to operate through a local agent. G is concerned to appoint a reputable agent and ensure that the risk of bribery being used to develop its business in the market is minimised.

G could consider any or a combination of the following:

- Compiling a suitable questionnaire for potential agents requiring for example, details of ownership if not an individual; CVs and references for those involved in performing the proposed service; details of any directorships held, existing partnerships and third party relationships and any relevant judicial or regulatory findings.
- Having a clear statement of the precise nature of the services offered, costs, commissions, fees and the preferred means of remuneration.
- Undertaking research, including internet searches, of the prospective agents and, if a corporate body, of every person identified as having a degree of control over its affairs.

- Making enquiries with the relevant authorities in H to verify the information received in response to the questionnaire.
- Following up references and clarifying any matters arising from the questionnaire or any other information received with the agents, arranging face to face meetings where appropriate.
- Requesting sight or evidence of any potential agent's own anti-bribery policies and, where a corporate body, reporting procedures and records.
- Being alert to key commercial questions such as:
  - Is the agent really required?
  - Does the agent have the required expertise?
  - Are they interacting with or closely connected to public officials?
  - Is what you are proposing to pay reasonable and commercial?
- Renewing due diligence enquiries on a periodic basis if an agent is appointed.

Case Study 7 – Principle 5
Communicating and training

A small UK manufacturer of specialist equipment ('J') has engaged an individual as a local agent and adviser ('K') to assist with winning a contract and developing its business in a foreign country where the risk of bribery is assessed as high.

J could consider any or a combination of the following:

- Making employees of J engaged in bidding for business fully aware of J's anti-bribery statement, code of conduct and, where appropriate, that details of its anti-bribery policies are included in its tender.
- Including suitable contractual terms on bribery prevention measures in the agreement between J and K, for example: requiring K not to offer or pay bribes; giving J the ability to audit K's activities and expenditure; requiring K to report any requests for bribes by officials to J; and, in the event of suspicion arising as to K's activities, giving J the right to terminate the arrangement.
- Making employees of J fully aware of policies and procedures applying to relevant issues such as hospitality and facilitation payments,

including all financial control mechanisms, sanctions for any breaches
of the rules and instructions on how to report any suspicious conduct.
- Supplementing the information, where appropriate, with specially
  prepared training to J's staff involved with the foreign country.

Case Study 8 – Principle 1, 4 and 6
Community benefits and charitable donations

A company ('L') exports a range of seed products to growers around the
globe. Its representative travels to a foreign country ('M') to discuss with a
local farming cooperative the possible supply of a new strain of wheat that
is resistant to a disease which recently swept the region. In the meeting, the
head of the co-operative tells L's representative about the problems which
the relative unavailability of antiretroviral drugs cause locally in the face
of a high HIV infection rate.

In a subsequent meeting with an official of M to discuss the approval of
L's new wheat strain for import, the official suggests that L could pay for the
necessary antiretroviral drugs and that this will be a very positive factor in
the Government's consideration of the licence to import the new seed strain.
In a further meeting, the same official states that L should donate money
to a certain charity suggested by the official which, the official assures, will
then take the necessary steps to purchase and distribute the drugs. L identifies this as raising potential bribery risks.

L could consider any or a combination of the following:

- Making reasonable efforts to conduct due diligence, including con-
  sultation with staff members and any business partners it has in
  country M in order to satisfy itself that the suggested arrangement
  is legitimate and in conformity with any relevant laws and codes
  applying to the foreign public official responsible for approving the
  product. It could do this by obtaining information on:
  - M's local law on community benefits as part of Government
    procurement and, if no particular local law, the official status
    and legitimacy of the suggested arrangement
  - the particular charity in question including its legal status, its rep-
    utation in M, and whether it has conducted similar projects, and

- any connections the charity might have with the foreign official in question, if possible.
- Adopting an internal communication plan designed to ensure that any relationships with charitable organisations are conducted in a transparent and open manner and do not raise any expectation of the award of a contract or licence.
- Adopting company-wide policies and procedures about the selection of charitable projects or initiatives which are informed by appropriate risk assessments.
- Training and support for staff in implementing the relevant policies and procedures of communication which allow issues to be reported and compliance to be monitored.
- If charitable donations made in country M are routinely channelled through government officials or to others at the official's request, a red flag should be raised and L may seek to monitor the way its contributions are ultimately applied, or investigate alternative methods of donation such as official 'off-set' or 'community gain' arrangements with the government of M.
- Evaluation of its policies relating to charitable donations as part of its next periodic review of its anti-bribery procedures.

Case Study 9 – Principle 4
Due diligence of agents

A small UK company ('N') relies on agents in country ('P') from which it imports local high quality perishable produce and to which it exports finished goods. The bribery risks it faces arise entirely as a result of its reliance on agents and their relationship with local businessmen and officials. N is offered a new business opportunity in P through a new agent ('Q'). An agreement with Q needs to be concluded quickly.

N could consider any or a combination of the following:

- Conducting due diligence and background checks on Q that are proportionate to the risk before engaging Q; which could include:
  - making enquiries through N's business contacts, local chambers of commerce or business associations, or internet searches

- seeking business references and a financial statement from Q and reviewing Q's CV to ensure Q has suitable experience.
- Considering how best to structure the relationship with Q, including how Q should be remunerated for its services and how to seek to ensure Q's compliance with relevant laws and codes applying to foreign public officials.
- Making the contract with Q renewable annually or periodically.
- Travelling to P periodically to review the agency situation.

Case Study 10 – Principle 2
Top-level commitment

A small to medium sized component manufacturer is seeking contracts in markets abroad where there is a risk of bribery. As part of its preparation, a senior manager has devoted some time to participation in the development of a sector wide anti-bribery initiative.

The top-level management of the manufacturer could consider any or a combination of the following:

- The making of a clear statement disseminated to its staff and key business partners of its commitment to carry out business fairly, honestly and openly, referencing its key bribery prevention procedures and its involvement in the sectoral initiative.
- Establishing a code of conduct that includes suitable anti-bribery provisions and making it accessible to staff and third parties on its website.
- Considering an internal launch of a code of conduct, with a message of commitment to it from senior management.
- Senior management emphasizing among the workforce and other associated persons the importance of understanding and applying the code of conduct and the consequences of breaching the policy or contractual provisions relating to bribery prevention for employees and managers and external associated persons.
- Identifying someone of a suitable level of seniority to be a point-person for queries and issues relating to bribery risks.

Case Study 11
Proportionate procedures
A small export company operates through agents in a number of different foreign countries. Having identified bribery risks associated with its reliance on agents it is considering developing proportionate and risk based bribery prevention procedures.

The company could consider any or a combination of the following:

- Using trade fairs and trade publications to communicate periodically its anti-bribery message and, where appropriate, some detail of its policies and procedures.
- Oral or written communication of its bribery prevention intentions to all of its agents.
- Adopting measures designed to address bribery on its behalf by associated persons, such as:
  - requesting relevant information and conducting background searches on the internet against information received
  - making sure references are in order and followed up
  - including anti-bribery commitments in any contract renewal
  - using existing internal arrangements such as periodic staff meetings to raise awareness of 'red flags' as regards agents' conduct, for example evasive answers to straightforward requests for information, overly elaborate payment arrangements involving further third parties, ad hoc or unusual requests for expense reimbursement not properly covered by accounting procedures.
- Making use of any external sources of information (UKTI, sectoral organisations) on bribery risks in particular markets and using the data to inform relationships with particular agents.
- Making sure staff have a confidential means to raise any concerns about bribery.

Acknowledgments

I should like to acknowledge the help and expertise provided by my co-authors, Stuart and Truman, with whom it has been a real pleasure to work on this project.

I have also on occasion been assisted by reference to two books on the subject, namely THE BRIBERY ACT 2010: A PRACTICAL GUIDE by Eoin O'Shea (Jordan Publishing Limited 2011) and LISSACK AND HORLICK ON BRIBERY by Richard Lissack and Fiona Horlick (LexisNexis 2011).

Vivian Robinson

This joint effort has been a remarkably pleasant experience working with Vivian and Truman, two extremely able and thoughtful colleagues.

We very much appreciate the support in this endeavor of the American Bar Association's ('ABA') Section of International Law and ABA Publishing and their capable staffs. We similarly appreciate being able to draw upon my previous book: THE FOREIGN CORRUPT PRACTICES ACT AND THE NEW INTERNATIONAL NORMS (ABA Publishing 2010).

Stuart H. Deming

Throughout this effort, we have benefited from the time and assistance of many members of our family, friends and professional colleagues. Primary among those who provided invaluable support and assistance to me are my wife Fredericka, kids Tahlia, Talya and Taryn—my sources of inspiration. My family in Bahamas, Mother Mildred, Brother Garfield and Sister Sharmaine for dutifully tolerating my absence for extended periods.

Chanel Rowe, Jessica Battle and Derrick Raphael, who kept me focused with numerous points to consider on international anti-corruption enforcement. My employer Wells Fargo Law Department and colleagues on the (ASA) Anti-Money Laundering, Global Sanctions and Anti-Corruption team provided support that motivated me to continue.

Lastly, I owe a special word of thanks to my co-authors Vivian and Stuart, both of whom I greatly admire and respect for their knowledge, expertise and sheer good nature. I am honored to have been associated with you. I have thoroughly enjoyed our discussions and look forward to future collaboration.

Truman Kirkland Butler